Comyns Carr

Margaret Maliphant

Vol. I

Comyns Carr

Margaret Maliphant
Vol. I

ISBN/EAN: 9783337040994

Printed in Europe, USA, Canada, Australia, Japan

Cover: Foto ©ninafisch / pixelio.de

More available books at **www.hansebooks.com**

MARGARET MALIPHANT

A NOVEL

BY

MRS COMYNS CARR

AUTHOR OF 'LA FORTUNINA,' 'NORTH ITALIAN FOLK,' ETC.

IN THREE VOLUMES

VOL. I.

WILLIAM BLACKWOOD AND SONS
EDINBURGH AND LONDON
MDCCCLXXXIX

MARGARET MALIPHANT.

PROLOGUE.

It is twilight upon the marsh : the land at the foot of the hill lies a level of dim monotony, and even the sea beyond is lost in mystery. In the middle of the plain one solitary homestead, with its clump of trees, stands out just a little darker than anything else, and from afar there comes to me the sound of the sea, sweetly lulling, as it has come to me ever since I was a little child. A chill breeze creeps up among the aspens on the cliff, and for a moment there steals over me the sense of loneliness of ten years ago, and I seem to see once more a tall, dark figure thread his way down among the trees, and disappear for ever on to the wide plain. But this is only for a moment; for as I look, the past lies stretched, as the plain is stretched, before me—vivid, yet distant as a dream. The white mill detaches itself upon the dark hillside, the cattle rest upon the quiet marsh; and still the sound of the sea comes to me, tenderly murmuring, as it did when I was a happy child, and tells me of a present that is wide and fair as, above the lonely land, the coming Night is blue and vast.

CHAPTER I.

My sister Joyce is older than I am. At the time of which I am thinking she was twenty-one, and I was barely nineteen. We were the only children of Farmer Maliphant of Knellestone Grange, in the county of Sussex. The Maliphants were an old family. Their names were on the oldest tombstones in the graveyard of the Abbey, whose choir and ruined transepts were all that was left standing of a splendid church that had been the mother of a great monastery, and of many other churches in the Popish days, when our town was a feature in English history. I am not sure that our family dated as far back as that. I had read of knights in helmets and coats of mail skirmishing beneath the city wall, of which there were still fragments standing, and of gallant captains bringing the king's galleys to port in the bay that had become marshland, and I hoped that there might have been Maliphants too, riding up and down the hill under the gateways that were now ivy-grown; but I am afraid that, even if the family had been in existence at the time, they would only have been archers, shooting their arrows from behind the turrets on the hill.

At all events—to leave romancing alone—Maliphants had owned or rented land upon the Udimore hills and the downs of Brede for more than three hundred years, and it must have been nearly as long as that that they had lived in the old stone house overlooking the Romney Marsh. For almost all our land had been a manor of the old Abbey, and had been granted to my father's family at the dissolution of the monasteries in 1540, and it was not much more than a century since the Maliphants had been obliged to sell most of it to the ancestors of him who was now Squire at the big house. But they had never left the old home, renting the land that they had once owned, and tilling the soil that they had once been lords of. Our house was the oldest house in the place, antiquaries testifying to the fact that it was built of the same foreign stone that fashioned the walls of the old Abbey; and our name was the oldest name—a fact which my father, democrat as he was, never really forgot. But we were not so well-to-do as we had once been, even in the memory of living folk.

Family portraits of ladies in scanty gowns and high waists, and of gallants in ruffled shirts, made pleasant pictures in my fancy; and there were whispered stories of kegs of spirits stored at dead of night in the old cellars beneath the house in my grandfather's time, and of mother's old Mechlin lace having been brought, at the risk of bold lives, in the merry little fishing-smacks that defied the revenue cutters. But smuggling was a dead art in our time, and respectable folk would have been ashamed to buy smuggled goods. We lived the uneventful life of our neighbours, and were no longer the great people that we had been even in my grandfather's time; for farming was not now so lucrative.

My sister Joyce was very handsome. I

have not seen much of the world, but I am sure that any one would have said so. She was tall, taller than I am, and I am not short, and she was slight, and fair as a rose. There was a sort of gentle Quaker-like dignity about Joyce, which I have never seen in one so young. She had it of our mother. Both women were very tall, and both bore their height bravely. Sometimes, it is true, when Joyce walked along the dark passages of the old Grange, her arms full of sweet-scented linen, and bending her little head to pass under the low doorways, or when she made the jam in the kitchen, or pats of butter in the dairy, she stooped just a little over her work; but when—of a June evening—she would come across the lawn with her hands full of guelder-roses and peonies for the parlour, no one could have said that she was too tall, so erect and gracefully did she seem to flit across the earth.

Of course I did not consciously notice these things when I was nineteen; but as I think of her again now, I can see that it was not at all to be wondered at that the country-folk used to talk of Joyce Maliphant as a poor slip of a thing, not fit to be a countryman's wife. There was an over-sensitiveness about her—a sort of tremulous reserve—that marked her as belonging to a different order of beings. It was not that she was weak either in mind or in body. Joyce would often surprise one by her sudden purposes, and as for fatigue, that slender figure could work all day without being tired, and though the cheek was as dainty as the petal of a flower, it had nothing frail about it: it told of health, just as did the clearness of the blue eye and the wealth of the rippling auburn hair.

Joyce kept her complexion, partly because she was less out of doors than I was; but if I had known that I could have had her lovely skin instead of my own freckled face, I do not believe that I would have changed with her. No doubt mother was right, and I might have kept that—my one good point—if I had cared to. Red-haired people generally do have fresh skins, and my hair is just about the colour of Virginian creeper leaves in autumn, or of the copper kettle in the sunlight. I was very much ashamed of it in those days.

Luckily I gave little heed to my appearance. I was quite content to leave the monopoly of the family beauty to my sister, if I might have freedom to scour the marshland with Taff, the big St Bernard; and so long as my father treated me like a boy and let me help him superintend the farm, he might banter as much as he liked about "Margaret's grey eyes that looked a different colour every day," and even rail at me for heavy eyelids that didn't look a bit as if I led a healthy outdoor life. But I did: when there was neither washing nor baking nor butter-making to help with, I was out of doors from morning to night. When I was a child it was with Reuben Ruck the shepherd, and his black colley Luck, who was the best sheep-dog in the country.

Reuben taught me many things—where to find the forms of the hares upon the marshland, the nests of the butcher-birds and yellow-hammers and wheat-ears that were all peculiar to our home; he taught me to surprise the purple herons upon the sands or by the dykes at eventide, to find the peewit's eggs upon the shingle, to tame the squirrels in the Manor woods, to catch grey mullet in the Channel, to spear eels in the dykes, to know when every bird's brood came forth, to welcome the various arrivals of the swifts and martins and swallows.

At the time of which I write, Reuben had had to give up his shepherd's duties, owing to ill-health, and used to do odd jobs about the house and garden; but he had bred the love of the country in me, and now it was useless for mother to bemoan my wandering habits, or even for our old nurse, Deborah, to take me to task for not caring more about the home pursuits in which my sister so brilliantly excelled. Whatever related to a bird or a beast I would attend to with alacrity; but as for household duties, I only got them over as quickly as I could, that I might the sooner be out in the air. I knew every hill's crest inland, every headland out to sea, every shepherd's track across the marsh, every plank across the channels. The shepherds and the coastguards were all my friends alike, and I think there was not one of them who would not have braved danger rather than I should come to harm, although I do not suppose that I ever exchanged more than six words' conversation with any of them in all my life. Words were not necessary between us.

"Farmer Maliphant's little Miss" had always been a favourite, and "Farmer Maliphant's little Miss" was always his youngest daughter. I like to remember the title now; I like to remember that if Joyce was mother's right hand in the house, I was father's companion in the fields. I was very fond of father; I was very fond of any praise of his. I did not get on so well with mother. I suppose daughters often do not get on so well with their mothers. For though Joyce was a fresh, neat, deft girl, just after mother's own heart, and I know that she thought there was none to equal her, they never got on well together. I was always fighting her battles. She was too gentle, or too proud—I was never sure which—to fight them for herself. A cross word only spoken in the excitement of a domestic crisis—which meant worlds to a woman to whom housekeeping was an art—would shut Joyce up in an armour of reserve for days, and I often laughed at her even while I fought for her.

As for me, I used to think I could manage mother. I wish I had the dear old days back again! It's little managing I would care to do. It came to very little good. I believe that every quarrel I had for Joyce only did her harm with mother; I was such a headstrong girl that it took a deal to set me down, and I am afraid that she got some of the thrusts that were meant for me in consequence.

One of the special, though tacit, subjects of difference between mother and myself was upon the choice of a husband for my sister. I quite agreed with the country-folk—that she was not suited to be a countryman's wife —but I did not agree with mother's idea of a suitable husband for her.

Mother was a very ambitious woman. She wanted us to rise in the world; she wanted us to hold once more something of the position she knew the family had once held. She was not a highly educated woman herself, but she was a shrewd woman. She had had us educated to the best of her abilities, a little better than other farmers' daughters; if she had had her way, she would have sent me, as the cleverer, to school in London. But father would have none of it. He never denied her a whim for herself, but he did not hold with boarding-school learning.

I was left to finish my education by living my life. But mother was none the less ambitious for us, and being an old-fashioned woman, her ambition aspired to good marriages for us. And I—foolish girl that I was—chose to think that the particular man whom she hoped that Joyce's beauty would secure was a very commonplace lover, and not at all worthy of her. In the first place, he occupied a better position in the world than she did, and would probably consider that he was raising her by the marriage, which my pride resented. For, after all, it was only what the world considered a better position; he owned the land that we worked. But the land had only been bought by his ancestors; whereas our forefathers had owned it for more than two hundred years before that, so that we considered that we were of the finer stock.

As I set this down now in black and white, I smile to myself : it represents so very badly the real relations that existed between our two families, for the man of whom I speak has always been to us the best and stanchest of friends, and even at that time there was hearty simple intercourse between us, that was quite uninfluenced by difference of rank or party spirit. But the words express a certain side of our feelings, especially a certain side of my own particular feelings, and therefore they shall stand.

The man whom mother hoped Joyce might marry was Squire Broderick. Ever since we girls could remember, he had been Squire at the big house, for his father had died when he was scarcely twenty-one, and from that time he had been master of the thousand rooks that used to fly across the marsh at even, to their homes in the beeches and elms that sheltered the Manor from the sea-gales.

I remember thinking when I was a child that it was very strange the rooks should always fly to Squire Broderick's trees rather than to ours. For we had trees too, although not so many nor so big, and our house only stood at the other end of the hill, that sloped down on both sides into the marsh. His house was large and square and regular—a red-brick Elizabethan house—and had a great many more windows and chimneys than ours had, and a great many more flower-beds on the lawn that looked out across the marsh to the sea.

But although the Grange had been often added to in the course of its history, and was therefore irregular in shape and varied in colour, according to the time that the stone had stood the weather, or to the mosses and ivy that clung to its grey walls, I am sure that it was just as fine an old structure in its way, with its high-pitched tiled roof and the lattice windows, that only looked like eyes in the empty spaces of solid stone.

We certainly had a better view than the Squire. From the low windows of the front parlour we could see the red-roofed town rise, like a sentry-tower out of the plain, some three miles away; and, beyond the ruin of the round stone fortress, lying like a giant asleep in the tawny marshland, we looked across the wide stretch of flat pasture-land to the storms and the blue of the sea in the distance.

I do not suppose that I was conscious of the strange beauty of this marshland as I am conscious of it now; but I know that I loved it—though people do say that country-folk have no admiration of nature—and I know that I was glad that we saw more of it than they did from the Manor, where a belt of trees had been allowed to grow up and shut out the view. But the rooks loved that lordly belt of trees, and I think that, as a child, I envied the Squire the rooks. If I did, it was the only thing I ever did envy him.

As the child of the Squire's tenant, and proud of my family pride, it was born in me rather to dislike him than otherwise for his fine old house and his many acres. But this was only when something occurred to remind me of these sentiments — to wit, mother's desire for a marriage between my sister and the village big-wig. Otherwise I did not think of him in this light at all, but rather as the provider of the only treats that ever came our way in that quiet life; for it was he who would make up a party to take us to the travelling shows in the little town when they came by, or even sometimes to the larger seaport ten miles off. I can still remember the school feasts at the Manor when we were little girls, and the Squire had but just come into his own, and how, when the village tea and cake had been handed round, he would take us two all over the grounds alone, and give us lovely posies of hothouse flowers to take back to the Grange parlour.

I can even recollect a ride on his back round the field when I tried to catch the pony, and how wildly I laughed all the time, making the meadows ring with my merriment; but that must have been when I was scarcely more than five years old. Since then he had been a husband and a father, and now he was a widower, and in my eyes quite an old man, although, I suppose, he can have been little more than five-and-thirty.

I do not remember Mrs Broderick. I asked mother about her once, and she told me that she had died when I was scarcely ten years old. And from our old servant,

Deborah, I had further gleaned that it was in giving birth to a little son, who had died a year after her, and that mother could not bear to speak of it, because it was just at the same time that we lost our little brother John. Both children had died of scarlet fever, and mother had nursed the Squire's motherless boy before her own. I suppose that was why the Squire was always so tender and reverential to her.

I know I was sorry for the Squire; for it seemed hard he should have no heir to all his acres, and should have to live in that big house all alone. But he did not seem to mind it much: he was always cheery; his fair fresh face always with a smile on it; his frank blue eyes always bright. It did one good to see him; it was like a breath of fresh air. I think everybody felt the same thing about him. It was not only that he was generous, a just landlord, "always as good as his word"—there was something more in it than that; there was something that made everybody love him, apart from anything that he did. And as I look back now to the past, I can see that the Squire can have had no easy time of it amongst the people. He had a thorn in the flesh, and that thorn was my father.

The Squire was an ardent Conservative, and father was—well, whatever he was, he was opposed to the Squire; and as he was one of those people who have the rare gift of imparting their convictions and their enthusiasms to others, he had great influence among the working classes, and his influence was not favourable to the Squire's party. And yet father was no politician. I knew nothing about shades in these matters at that time, and because father was not a Tory I imagined that he must be a Liberal. But he was not a Liberal, still less was he a Radical, in the party sense of the word. As I have said, he belonged to no party. The reforms that he wanted were social reforms, and they could only be won by the patient struggles of the people who required them. That was what he used to say, and I suppose that was why he devoted all his strength to encouraging the working classes, and cared so little for their existing rulers. But I did not understand this at the time; it was not till long afterwards that I appreciated all that my father was. Then it occurred to me to wonder how he had come by such advanced ideas living in a quiet country village, and I remembered of a sudden some words that he had said to me one day when I had asked him about a little crayon sketch that always hung above the writing-table in his business-room. It was the portrait of a young man with a firm square chin, a sensitive mouth, liquid fiery eyes. He wore his hair brushed back off his broad forehead, and had altogether a foreign air. It was a fascinating face.

"That, Meg," he had said, "was a great man—a man who made war against the strong, who helped the poor and downtrodden, and fought for the laws of justice and liberty. He gave his affections, his goods, his brains, and his life to the service of others. He died poor, but was rich. He was a real Christian. His name was Camille Lambert."

He said no more, and I never liked to broach the subject again; for mother had told me afterwards that he had had a romantic friendship for the young Frenchman shortly after her engagement to him, and that he could never bear to speak of him after the time when he laid him to rest under the shadows of the old Abbey Church.

Mother could tell me little about him beyond the fact that he was some years older than father, and that his parents had belonged to the remnants of that colony of French refugees who had inhabited our town during the last century, and still left their names to many existing houses. Indeed I thought no more of it at the time; but when long afterwards I remembered the matter, I hunted up a little manuscript pamphlet in father's handwriting, telling the story of his friend's life.

Camille Lambert was a disciple of St Simon who had died when my father was yet but a lad. Of an eager and romantic temperament, his enthusiasm had been early fired by those exalted doctrines, and he had given all his substance to the great "school," which had just opened its branch houses in the provinces.

In all the works connected with it, Camille

Lambert had taken an active part; and when financial troubles and dissensions between the leaders led popular ardour to cool and the scheme to be declared unpractical, he broke his heart over the failure of his hopes, and came home to the little English village to die.

As I read those pages in after years, I felt that it was no wonder that such an enthusiasm should have kindled a kindred flame in the heart of a man so just and so tender as I knew my dear father to be. I love to think of that friendship now; it explains a great deal to me which has sometimes been a puzzle, when I have looked at my father's character with the more mature eyes of my present years. But in those days I did not think deeply enough for anything to be a puzzle. I was proud of my father's influence among the country-folk; I liked to hear the shouts of applause with which he was greeted when he stood up to speak at winter evening assemblies in the old Town Hall. I knew that the crusade he preached was that of the poor against the rich; and a confusion had arisen in my mind as to our attitude towards the Squire. I fancied I noticed a restive feeling in father towards the man to whom he paid the rent of his land; and when I guessed at that secret hope in mother's heart, I began to class the Squire with "the rich" against whom he waged war in theory, and forgot the many occasions in which they were one at heart in the performance of kindly and generous actions.

My mood did not last long; for the old habit of a lifetime was stronger than a mood, and the Squire was our friend,—but for the moment that was my mood. The Squire belonged to an antagonistic class; perhaps, even worse than that in my eyes, he was a middle-aged man, and Joyce must not marry him. Mother never spoke of her hopes to me. It was old Deborah who sometimes discussed them,—she always did discuss the family concerns far more freely than any one else in the house. She was with us when Joyce was born, and it was natural she should talk most of what mattered to those whom she loved most in the world. But Deborah could not be expected to enter into the delicacy of such a situation, and I felt sure that on me fell the duty of fighting to the death before my beautiful sister should be sacrificed to commonplace affluence, instead of shining in the world of romance that I loved to fancy for her.

CHAPTER II.

CAPTAIN FORRESTER was the hero of the romance that I had fashioned in my head for Joyce. One bright, frosty winter's day I had driven her into town to market. The sky was blue, the air was sharp, the little icicles hung glittering from the trees and hedgerows as we drove down the hill; the sea lay steely and calm beyond the waste of white marshland that looked so wide in its monotony. The day was invigorating to the spirits, and it had the same effect on father's new mare as it had on us; the road, besides, was as hard as iron and very slippery.

Joyce was nervous in a dog-cart, and she had her doubts of the new purchase. For the matter of that, so had I. The mare pulled very hard. However, we got into town well enough, and in the excitement of her purchases Joyce forgot her uneasiness. It was a long time before she was quite suited to her mind in the matter of soap, and ham, and kitchen utensils; and just as we were leaving I remembered that mother had told me to bring her some tapes and needles.

"I've forgotten something, Joyce," said I. "Get in a minute and take the reins. I'll call a boy to hold the horse's head."

She got in, and I beckoned a lad hard by, who went to the animal's head. But before I had been in the shop a moment a cry from Joyce called me back. The mare was rearing. Whether the lad had teased her or not I do not know, but the mare was rearing, and at her head, instead of the lad I had called, was Captain Forrester. We did not know what his name was then; we merely saw a tall, good-looking man in smarter clothes than were usually worn by the dandies of the neighbourhood, soothing the restless animal, who soon showed that she recognised a friend. Joyce was as white as a sheet; but when the young man turned to me and said, raising his hat, "Miss Joyce

Maliphant, I believe," she blushed as red as a poppy.

It was strange that he should know her name so well.

"No," said I, "I am not Joyce; I am Margaret Maliphant. My sister's name is Joyce."

I waved towards her as I spoke. Perhaps I was a little offhand; folk say I always am. I suppose I must have been, for he muttered a half apology.

"I should not have ventured to intrude," said he, "but that I know the nature of this animal. Strangely enough, she belonged to me once. She is not suitable for a lady's driving."

"Why," said I, puzzled and half-doubtful, "father only bought her last week from Squire Broderick."

"Exactly," smiled he, and I noticed what a pleasant, genial smile he had. "I sold the mare to Squire Broderick myself. I know him very well."

"Oh!" ejaculated I, I am afraid still far from graciously.

He was still standing by the horse, stroking its neck.

"Yes," he repeated, and his tone was not a jot less pleasant because I had spoken so very ungraciously. "She used to belong to me. She has a bit of a temper."

"I like a horse with a little temper," answered I. "A horse that has a hard mouth is dull driving."

I said it out of pure intent to brag, for I had been offended at its being supposed I could not drive any horse. As I spoke, I put my foot on the step to mount the dog-cart. As soon as the mare felt the movement behind her she reared again slightly. Captain Forrester quieted her afresh, but still there was no doubt about it, she had reared.

"Oh, Margaret," sighed Joyce, "I'm sure we shall never get home safely!"

"Nonsense!" cried I, impatiently.

I hated to have Joyce seem as though she mistrusted my power of managing a restive horse, and I hated equally to have her show herself off as a woman with nerves. I had already got up into my place, and I now took the reins from her hands and prepared to give the mare her head.

"I think I shall walk, Margaret," said Joyce, in a voice which I knew meant that there would be no persuading her from her purpose. She was not generally obstinate, but when she was frightened she would not listen to any reason.

Rather than have a scene, I knew it would be best to give in.

"Very well; then we will both walk," said I. "You had better get down, and I will drive on and put the cart up at the inn. Reuben will have to walk out this evening and take it home."

I know I spoke crossly; it was wrong, but I was annoyed. However, even before Joyce had had time to get down I saw that our new friend had gone round to the other side of the dog-cart and was talking to her.

"Miss Maliphant," said he—and I could not help remarking what a charming manner he had, and what a fascinating way of fixing his wide-open light-brown eyes full in the face of the person to whom he was speaking, and yet that without anything bold in the doing of it—"Miss Maliphant, will you let me drive you and your sister home? I know how uncomfortable it is to be nervous, and I don't think you would be frightened if I were driving, for, you see, I understand the mare quite well."

Joyce blushed, and I bit my lip. It certainly was very mortifying to have a perfect stranger setting himself up as a better whip than I was.

Joyce answered. "Oh, thank you, I don't think we could trouble you to do that," she said, with a bend of her pretty head.

"It would be no trouble," replied he, looking at her. "I am going in your direction." He did not say it eagerly, only with a pleasant smile as though his offer were made out of pure politeness.

I looked at him. He was young and handsome, and he was most certainly a gentleman, for he had the most perfect and easy manners that I had ever met with in any man; and he was looking at Joyce as I fancied a man might look at the woman whom he could love. Suddenly all my offence at his want of respect to my powers of driving evaporated. For a thought flashed across my mind. Might this be the lover of whom I had dreamed for my beautiful sister? He had learnt her name beforehand; therefore he must have seen her, and also have been sufficiently attracted by her to wish to find out who she was.

Why, was it not possible that he had fallen in love with her at first sight, and that he had sought this opportunity of knowing her? Such things had been known to happen, and Joyce was certainly beautiful enough to account for any ardour in an admirer. I stood a moment undecided myself. A young man from the shop where I had made my little purchase came out and put the parcel in the dog-cart. He held another in his hand.

"This is for the Manor, Captain," said he. "Shall I put it in the carriage?"

"No, no, thank you," answered our new friend. "The Squire will be driving over one of these days and will fetch it."

This settled the question for me.

"Captain!"

There was something so much more romantic about a Captain than about a plain Mister. And such a Captain! I had met captains before at the Volunteer ball, but not like this one. It did not occur to me for a moment that if the gentleman was a friend of the Squire's he must needs belong to the class which I thought I abhorred, and therefore should not be a suitable lover for my sister. I was too much fascinated by the individual to remember the class. Joyce looked at me for help.

"I don't know what to say, I'm sure," murmured she.

The horse began to fidget again at being kept so long standing. There could be no possible objection to a friend of the Squire's driving us over.

"Thank you," said I, trying to be cool and dignified and not at all eager. "If you would be so kind as to drive us, I shall be very much obliged to you." And turning to the shop-boy, I added, "Put the parcel into the carriage."

I do not know what the Captain must have thought of my sudden change of manner; I did not stop to consider. I jumped to the ground before he had time to help me, and began to let down the back seat of the cart.

"No, no; don't leave the horse," cried I, as he came round to the back to help me. "I know how to do this perfectly well. Do get up. Joyce is so very nervous."

"As you like," said he, still smiling; and he got up beside Joyce.

In a moment I had fixed the seat and jumped into it, and we started off at a smart trot down the village street. Joyce was not entirely reassured, although vanity prevented her from openly expressing her alarm, as she would have done if I had been at her side. She sat holding on to the cart, with lips parted and eyes fixed on the horse's ears. I had turned round a little on the seat so that I could see her, and I thought that she looked very lovely. I thought Captain Forrester must be of the same mind; but I think he had not much time to look at her just then—the mare kept his hands full. We rattled down the hill over the cobble-stones and out of the town. Soon its red roofs, crowned by the square tower of the ancient church at its summit, were only a feature in the landscape, which I watched gradually mellowing into the white background as I sat with my back to the others. Before long I was lost in one of what father would have called my brown studies, and quite forgot to notice whether the two in front of me were getting on well together or not. The vague dream that I had always had about my sister's future was beginning to take shape— it unrolled itself slowly before me in a sweet and delightful picture, to which the fair scene before me imparted life and brilliancy as the sense of it mingled imperceptibly with my thoughts. I had never known what it really was that I desired for my sister's lot. To be the wife of a country bumpkin she was far too beautiful; and yet I thought that nothing should have induced me to help towards mating her with one of the gentry who crushed the people's honest rights. Sir Walter Scott's 'Fair Maid of Perth,' which I had just finished reading, had lent wings to my youthful imagination; but there were no burghers in these days who held the honourable positions of those smiths and glovers, although no doubt at that time there had been many such living in the very town where we had just been to market, and which was in days of old one of the strongholds of his Majesty's realm. If there had been any such suitors, I think I would have given our "Fair Maid" to one of them; but there was all the difference between the man who owned the linen-draper's shop—even if he did not measure off yards of stuff behind the counter—and the man who fashioned the goods with his own hand and took a pride in making them beautiful. And nowadays there were no men who made armour—there were no men who needed it. War had become a very brutal thing compared to what it was then, when it really was a trial of individual strength; nevertheless, of the professions of which I knew anything, it was still to my mind the finest, and it seemed to me that a fine profession was the only thing between a countryman and a landed proprietor such as Squire Broderick. I wonder if I should have thought all this out so neatly if the fine, handsome, and gentlemanly young man who had come across our path had not borne the title of "Captain"? Any way, it had struck my fancy, as he had struck my fancy—for Joyce.

There was something fresh, and brave,

and bright about him, with those wide-open brown eyes, that he fixed so intently upon one's own. I felt sure that he was full of enthusiasm, full of courage and of loyalty—every inch a soldier. He was the first man I had ever seen who impressed me by his personality; and yet with all that, he was so simple, so light and easy.

As I look back now upon my first impression of Captain Forrester, I do not think it was an unnatural one. I think that he really had a rare gift of fascination, and it was not to be wondered at that I said to myself that this was the noble hero of whom I had dreamed that he should carry off the lily nurtured in the woodland shade. He was just the kind of man to fit in with my notion of a gallant and a hero—a notion derived solely from those old-fashioned novels of father's library which I devoured in the secrecy of my bedchamber when I could snatch a moment from household darning, and mother was not by to pass her scathing remarks upon even such profitable romance-reading as the works of Sir Walter Scott and Jane Austen.

As I sat there in the midst of the snow-plain, with the ocean beyond it, and the weather-worn old town the only human thing in the wide landscape, I fixed my thoughts upon that one little spot with all the concentration of my nature, and fell to weaving a romance far more brilliant than anything I had read, or than anything that had yet suggested itself to me in my quiet everyday life. The days of gay tournaments, and fierce hand-to-hand combats, and warriors clad in suits of mail, were no longer; but still, to fight for one's country's fame, to win one's bread by adventure and glory, to kill one's country's foes and save the lives of her sons, was the grandest thing that could be, I thought; and this Captain Forrester did.

As I dreamed, my eyes grew dim thinking of the wife who must send her lover from her, perhaps for ever—even though it be to glorious deeds; and as I dreamed, the dog-cart gave a jolt over a stone, and I awoke from my foolish fancies to see that Captain Forrester's hard driving had taken all the mischief out of the mare, and that she was

trotting along quite peaceably, while he let
the reins hang loose upon her neck, and
turned round to talk to my sister Joyce.
And as we passed the clump of tall elms
at the foot of the cliff, and began slowly to
climb the hill towards the village, I looked
out across the cold expanse of white marshland to the calm sea beyond, and wondered
whether it were true what the books said that
the peace of a perfect love could only be won
through trouble and heartache. Any way,
the trouble must be worth the reward, since
we all admired those who fought for it, and
most of us entered the lists ourselves. But
no doubt the trouble and the fighting was
always on the man's side, and as I caught a
glimpse of Joyce's blushing profile and of the
Captain's eager gaze, I said to myself that
Joyce was beautiful, and that Joyce was
sweet, and that Joyce would have a lover to
whom no trouble in the whole world would
be too much for the sake of one kiss from
her lips.

CHAPTER III.

I HAD jumped down as we ascended the hill, and had walked by the side of the cart. Captain Forrester had turned round now and then to say a word to me, making pleasant general remarks upon the beauty of the country and the healthiness of the situation. But he did it out of mere politeness, I knew well enough. When we reached the top of the hill, he gave the reins to Joyce and got down.

"You'll be all right now, won't you?" said he, helping me in. "I won't come to the door, for I'm due at home;" and he nodded in the direction of the Manor.

Then he must be staying in our village.

I said aloud, laughing, "Well, we could hardly get into trouble between this and our house, could we?"

"Hardly," laughed he back again, looking down the road to the right, which led to the ivied porch of our house.

How well he seemed to know all about us! Was he the Squire's guest as well as his friend? If so, Joyce would see him again.

"Won't you come in and see my father and mother?" said I.

I was not sure whether it was the thing to do in good society, such as that to which I felt instinctively that he belonged, but I knew that it was the hospitable thing to do, and I did it. Joyce seconded my invitation in an inarticulate murmur.

I think we were both of us considerably relieved when he said with that same gay smile, and speaking with his clear, well-bred accent, "Not now, thank you. But I will come and call very soon, if I may."

He added the last words turning round to Joyce. She blushed and looked uncomfortable. We were both thinking that mother might possibly not welcome this stranger so cordially as we had done. However, I was not going to have this good beginning spoilt by any mistake on my part, and I hastened to say, "Oh yes, pray do come. I am sure mother will be delighted to welcome any friend of Squire Broderick's."

He gave a little bow at that, but he did not say anything. He held out his hand to me, and then turned to Joyce. I fancied that hers rested in his just a moment longer than was necessary; but then I was in the mood to build up any romance at the moment, and no doubt I was mistaken. But anyhow, I turned the dog-cart down rather sharply towards the house, and Captain Forrester had to stand aside. I was not going to have the villagers gossiping; and such a thing had not been seen before, as Farmer Maliphant's two daughters talking with a stranger at the corner of the village street.

"I wonder whether he is staying at the Manor," said I, as we drove up the gravel.

And Joyce echoed, "I wonder."

But she had plenty to do when she got in, showing her new purchases to mother, and telling her the market prices of household commodities, and I do not suppose that she gave a thought to her new admirer for some time. At all events she did not speak of him. Neither did I. I did not go indoors.

I always was an unnatural sort of a girl in some ways, and shopping and talk about shopping never interested me. I preferred to remain in the yard, and discuss the points of the new mare with Reuben. But all the time, I was thinking of the man whom we had met in town, and wondering whether or no he would turn out to be Joyce's lover. As I have said before, Reuben and I were great friends. He was a gaunt, loose-limbed old fellow, with a refined although by no means a handsome face, thin features, a fair pale skin, with white whiskers upon it. In character he was simple, obstinate, and taciturn, and had a queer habit of applying the same tests to human beings as he did to dumb animals. In the household—although every one respected his knowledge of his own business—I think that he was regarded merely as an honest, loyal nobody. It was only I who used sometimes to think that it was not all obtuseness, but also a laudable desire for a quiet life, which led Reuben to be such an easy mark for Deborah's wit, and apparently so impervious to its arrows.

"She pulled, did she!" said he, with a smile that showed a very good set of teeth for an old man. "Ah, it takes a man to hold a mare, leastways if she's got any spirit in her."

"She didn't pull any too much for me," answered I, half vexed. "What makes you fancy so?"

"I seed the young dandy a-driving ye along the road," said he. "I can see a long way. She pulled at first, but he took it out of her."

If there was any secret in our having driven out of town with Captain Forrester, Reuben had it.

"Joyce was frightened, and he had driven the mare at the Squire's," said I. "She reared a bit in the town, but I don't think he drove any better than I could have done."

Reuben took no notice of this remark. "She's a handsome mare," said he. "The handsomer they be, the worse they be to drive. Women are the same—so I've heard tell; though, to be sure, the ugly ones are bad enough."

Deborah was not handsome; but then, had Reuben ever tried to drive her? Oh, if she could have heard that speech! She came up the garden cliff in front of us as I spoke, with some herbs in her arms—a tall, strong woman, with a wide waist and shoulders, planting her foot firmly on the ground at every step, and swaying slightly on her hips with the bulk of her person. When she was young she must have had a fine figure, but now she was not graceful.

"Yes, she's a beauty," said I, stroking the mare's sleek sides, and alluding to her and not to Deborah. "When we are alone together we'll have fine fun." The mare stretched out her pretty neck to take the sugar that I held in my hand. She was beginning to know me already.

"Yes, Miss Joyce is nervous," said Reuben meditatively. "Most like she *would* have more confidence in a beau. Them pretty maids are that way, and the beaus buzz about them like flies to the honey.

But the beasts be fond of you, miss," he added admiringly, watching me fondling the horse.

It was the higher compliment from Reuben, and it was true that every animal liked me. I could catch the pony in the field when it would let no one else get near it. I could milk the cow who kicked over the pail for any one but Deborah. I could coax the rabbits to me, and almost make friends with the hares in the woods. The cat slept upon my bed, and Taff watched outside my door.

I laughed at Reuben's compliment; but Deborah strode out of the back-door just then, to hang linen out to dry, and Reuben never laughed when she was by. She gave me a sharp glance.

"You've got your frock out at the gathers again," said she. She did not often trouble to give us our titles of "Miss."

"Have I?" replied I carelessly.

"Yes, you have; and how you manage it is more than I can tell," continued she tartly. "Now you're grown up, I should think you might have done with jumping dykes, and riding horses without saddles, and such-like."

"Why, Deb," cried I, laughing, "I haven't jumped a dyke since I was fourteen. At least, not when any one was by," added I, remembering a private exploit of two days ago.

"Yes; I suppose you don't expect me not to know where that black mud came from on your petticoat last night," remarked she sententiously. "Anyhow, I'd advise you to mend your frock, for the Squire's in the parlour, and your mother won't be pleased."

"The Squire!" cried I. "Is he going to stay to dinner?"

"Not as I know of," answered the old woman. "But you had better go and see. Joyce let him in, for I hadn't a clean apron, and I heard him say that he had come to see the master on business."

"Well, so I suppose he did," answered I.

Deborah smiled, a superior sort of smile. She did not say anything, but I knew very well what she meant. She was the only person in the house who openly insisted that the Squire came to the Grange after Joyce.

Mother may have thought it; I guessed from many little signs that she did think it, but she never directly spoke of it. But Deborah spoke of it, and spoke of it frankly.

It irritated me. I pushed past her roughly to reach the front parlour windows. I wanted to see the Squire to-day, for I wanted to find out whether our new friend was staying at the Manor.

"You're never going in like that?" cried she.

"Certainly," replied I. "What's good enough for other folk is good enough for the Squire. The Squire is nothing to me, nothing at all."

"That's true enough," laughed Deborah. "I don't know as he is anything to you. But he may be something to other folk all the same. And look here, Miss Spitfire, there may come a day, for all your silly airs, when you may be glad enough that the Squire is something to some of you, and when you'd be very sorry if you'd done anything to prevent it. You go and think that over."

I curled my lip in scorn. "You know I

refuse to listen to any insinuations, Deborah," said I. "The Squire comes here to visit my father, and we have no reason to suppose that he comes for anything else."

This was quite true. The Squire had certainly never said a word that should lead us to imagine that he meant anything more by his visits to the Grange than friendship for an old man laid by from his active life by frequent attacks of gout; but if I had been quite honest, I should have acknowledged that I too entertained the same suspicion as Deborah did.

"The women must always needs be thinking the men be coming after them," muttered Reuben, emerging from the darkness of a shed to the left with an axe over his shoulder.

If I had been less preoccupied I should have laughed at the audacity of this remark, which he would certainly not have dared to make unless it had been for the support of my presence.

"It don't stand to reason," went on Deborah, scorning Reuben's remark, "that a gentleman like the Squire would come here and sit hours long for naught but to hear the gentry folk abused by the master. It is a wonder he stands it as he do, for master is over-unreasonable at times. But, Lord! you can't look in the Squire's eyes and not know he's got a good heart, and it's Miss Joyce's pretty face that'll get it to do what she likes with, you may take my word for it. The men they don't look to the mind so much as they look to the face and the temper—and Joyce, why, her temper's as smooth as her skin; you can't say better than that."

This was true, and Deborah was right to say it in praise, although I do believe in her heart she had even a softer spot for me and my bad temper than for Joyce and her gentle ways.

Birds of a feather, I suppose.

"You seem to think that it's quite an unnatural thing for two men to talk politics together, Deborah," said I, with a superior air of wisdom. "But perhaps the Squire is wiser than you fancy, and thinks that at his time of life politics should be more in his way than pretty faces."

Deborah laughed, quite good-humouredly this time.

"Hark at the lass!" cried she. "The time may come when you won't think a man of five-and-thirty too old to look at a woman, my dear."

"Oh, *I* don't mind how old a man is!" laughed I merrily, recovering my good-humour at the remembrance of that second string I had to my bow for my sister. "The men don't matter much to me—they never look twice at me, you know well enough. But Joyce is too handsome to marry an old widower, and I daresay if she waits a bit there'll come somebody by who'll be better suited to her."

"Well, all I can say is, I hope she may have another chance as good," insisted the obstinate old thing, shaking out the last stocking viciously and hanging it on to the line. "But she hasn't got it yet, you know; and if folk all behave so queer and snappish, maybe she won't have it at all. But you must all please yourselves," added she, as though she washed her hands of us now. And then giving me another of her sharp glances, she said in conclusion, "And you know whether your mother will like to see you with a torn frock or not."

I went in with my head in the air. I thought it was very impertinent of Deb to talk of "good chances" in connection with my sister. I have learned to know her better since then.

Her desire for that marriage was not all ambition for Joyce. But at that time I little guessed what she already scented in the air.

CHAPTER IV.

IT was a quarter of an hour before I reached the parlour, for I did mend my frock in spite of my bit of temper. The cloth was laid for dinner—a spotless cloth, for mother was very particular about her table-linen—and the bright glass and the dinner-ware shone in the sunlight. I can see the room now: a long, low room, with four latticed windows abreast, and a seat running the length of the windows; opposite the windows a huge fireplace, across which ran one heavy oaken beam bearing the date and the name of the Maliphants, and supported by two stout masonry pillars, fashioned, tradition said, out of that same soft stone of which a great part of the Abbey was built. Two high-backed wooden chairs, with delicate spindle rails, highly polished, and very elegant, stood close to the blaze. There was also a pretty inlaid satin-wood table in the far corner that had belonged to mother's grandfather, and had been left to her; but the rest of the furniture was plain, dark oak, and had been in the house ever since the Maliphants had owned it. It was a sweet, cosy room; and if the windows, being old-fashioned and somewhat small, did not admit all the sunlight they might, they also did not let in the wind, of which there was plenty, for the parlour faced towards the sea, and the gales in winter were sometimes terrific.

We had another best-parlour, looking on the road, where was the piano and the upholstered furniture, covered in brown holland on common days; but though the pale-yellow tabaret chairs and curtains looked very pretty when they were all uncovered, we none of us ever felt quite comfortable excepting in the big dwelling-room that looked over the marsh. How well I remember it that day when we were all there together! Father sat by the fire with his boots and gaiters still on. He had been out for the first time after a severe attack of his complaint, and he was very irritable. I thought Joyce might have helped him off with the heavy things, but no doubt he had refused; any offer of help was almost an insult to him. They used to say I took after father in that. He was bending over the fire that day, stretching out his fingers to the blaze—a powerful figure still, though somewhat worn with hard work and the sufferings which he never allowed to gain the upper hand. But his back was not bent—an outdoor life, whatever other marks it may leave, spares that one; his head was erect still — a remarkable head, — the grey hair, thick and strong, sticking up in obstinate little tufts without any attempt at order or smoothness. It was not beautiful hair, for the tufts were quite straight, but at least it was very characteristic; I have never seen any quite like it. It was in keeping with the bushy eyebrows, that had just the same defiant expression as the tufts of hair. The brow was high and prominent, the eyes keen and quick to change, the jaw heavy and somewhat sullen. At first sight it might not have been called a lovable face; it might rather have been called a stern, even an unbending one. But that it was really lovable, is proved by the sure love and confidence with which it always inspired little children. They came to father naturally as they would have gone to the tenderest woman, and smiled in his face as though certain beforehand of the smile that would answer theirs in return. But father's face was sullen sometimes to a grown-up person. It looked very sullen as he sat by the fire that day. I knew in a moment that something had ruffled him.

Mother seemed to be doing her best, however, to make up for the ill reception which her husband was giving his guest; and mother's best was a very pretty thing. She was a very pretty woman, and she looked her prettiest that day. She was tall—we were a tall family, I was the shortest of us all—and her height looked even greater than it was in the straight folds of the soft grey dress that suited so well with her fair skin. She had a fresh white cap on; the soft fluted frills came down in straight lines just below her ears, framing her face; and the bands of snow-white hair, that looked so pretty beside the fresh skin, were tucked away smoothly beneath it. Mother's face was a young face still—as dainty in colour as a little child's. Joyce took her beauty from her.

Mother was standing up in the middle of the room talking to the Squire, who apparently was about to take his leave. Joyce was putting the last touches to the dinner-table. She looked up at me in an appealing kind of way as I came in, and I felt sure that there had been some sort of difference between father and the Squire. They often did have little differences, though they were the best of friends in reality; but I always secretly took father's side in every argument, and I never liked to see mother, as it were, making amends for what father had said. Yet it was what she was doing now. "I'm sure, Squire Broderick," she was saying, "we take it very kindly of you to interest yourself in our affairs. Laban is a little tetchy just now, but it's because he ain't well. He feels just as I do, really."

Father made an impatient sound with his lips at this, but mother went on just the same.

"I'm quite of your mind," she declared, shaking her head. "I've often said so to Laban myself. We can't go against Providence, and we must learn to take help where we can get it, though I know ofttimes it's just the hardest thing we have to do."

What could this speech mean? I was puzzled. I glanced at father. He sat quite silent tapping his foot. I glanced at Joyce. There was nothing in her manner to show that the subject under discussion had anything whatever to do with her. The Squire had turned round as I came into the room, but mother kept him so to herself that he could do no more than give me a smile as I walked across and sat down in the window seat.

"I know it would be the best in the end," mother went on, with a distressed look on her sweet old face.

It rather annoyed me at the time, simply because I saw that she was siding with the Squire against father; but I have often remembered that, and many kindred looks since, and have wondered how it was that I never guessed at the anxiety of that tender spirit that laboured so devotedly to cope with problems that were beyond its grasp.

"However," added mother, with the pretty smile that, after all, I remember more often than the knitted brow, "he'll come round himself in time. He always does see things the way you put them after a bit."

She said these words in a whisper, although they were really quite loud enough for any one to hear. I saw father smile. He was so fond of mother, and the words were so far from accurate, that he could afford to smile; for there were very few instances in which he came round to the Squire's way of seeing things at that time, although he was very fond of the Squire. The Squire himself laughed aloud. He had a rich rippling laugh ; it did one good to hear it.

"No, no, ma'am," he said, "I can't agree to that. And no reason why it should be so either." He held out his hand to mother as he spoke.

"I must be off now," he added. "I ought to have gone long ago. We'll talk it over again another time."

"Oh, won't you stay and have a bit of

dinner with us, Squire," cried mother in a disappointed voice. "It's just coming in. I know it's not what you have at home, but it is a fine piece of roast-beef to-day."

"Fie, fie, Mrs Maliphant! don't you be so modest," said the Squire with his genial smile, buttoning up his overcoat as he spoke.

He always had a gay, easy manner towards the mother—something, I used to fancy, like her own younger brother might have had towards her, or even her own son, although at that time I should have thought it impossible for a man as old to be mother's son at all. I suppose it was in consequence of that sad time in the past that he had grown to love her as I know he did.

"I don't often get a dinner such as I get at your table," added he, "but I can't stay to-day, for I'm due at home."

Just the words that young man had used at the foot of the village street. I was determined to find out before the Squire left whether that young man was staying at the Manor or not.

"Perhaps Mr Broderick has visitors, mother," I suggested.

I glanced at Joyce as I spoke. Her cheeks were poppies.

"What makes you think so?" asked the Squire, turning to me and frowning a little.

"We met a gentleman in town," said I boldly, although my heart beat a little; "he helped us with the mare when she reared, and he said he was a friend of yours."

Mother looked at me, and Joyce blushed redder than ever. Certainly, for a straightforward and simple young woman who had no more than her legitimate share of vanity, Joyce had a most unfortunate trick of blushing. I know it was admired, but I never could see that folk must needs be more delicate of mind because they blushed, or more sensitive of heart because they cried. The Squire frowned a little more and bit his lip.

"Ah, it must have been Frank," said he. "He did say he was going to walk into town this morning. My nephew," added he in explanation, turning to mother. "Captain Forrester."

"Your nephew!" exclaimed mother, quite reassured. "He must be but a lad."

"Oh, not at all; he's a very well-grown

man, and of an age to take care of himself," answered the Squire, and it did not strike me then that he said it a little bitterly. "My sister is a great deal older than I am."

"Of course I have seen Mrs Forrester," said mother, "and I know she's a deal older than you are, but I never should have thought she had a grown-up son—and a captain, too!"

"Oh yes, he's a captain," repeated the Squire, and he took up his hat and stick from the corner of the room and put his hand on the door-knob. "Good-bye, Mr Maliphant," cried he cheerily, without touching any more on the sore subject.

Father did not reply, and he turned to me and held out his hand. "Good-bye," he said, more seriously than it seemed to me the subject required. "I'm sorry the mare reared."

"See the Squire to the door, Joyce," said the mother. And Joyce, blushing again, glided out into the hall and lifted the big latch.

CHAPTER V.

I WAS dying to hear what had been the subject of the difference between Squire Broderick and father, for that it was somehow related to something more closely allied to our own life than mere politics, I was inwardly convinced. I came up to the fireplace and began toasting my feet before the bars. I hoped father would say something. But he did not even turn to me, and Deborah coming in with the dinner at that moment, mother took her place at the head of the table, and father asked a blessing. Mother did not look sad; she looked very bright and pretty, with the sunshine falling on her silvery hair, and on her white dimpled hands, lovely hands, that were wielding the carvers so skilfully. I thought at the time that she did not notice father's gloomy face, but I think it is far more likely that she did notice it, but that she thought it wiser to leave him alone; those were always her tactics.

"Father," began she, as soon as she had served us all and had sat down, "the girls mustn't drive that mare any more if she rears,—it isn't safe."

"No, no, of course not," assented father absently. Then turning to me, "What made her rear, Meg?"

"I don't know, father," answered I. "I was in a shop when she did, and a boy was holding her. I suppose he teased her. But it's not worth talking about; it would have been nothing if Joyce hadn't been so easily frightened."

"I couldn't help it," murmured Joyce. "I know I'm silly."

"Well, to be sure, any old cart-horse would be better for you than a beast with any spirit, wouldn't it?" laughed I.

"Well, Margaret, the animal must have looked dangerous, you know," said mother, "for no strange gentleman would have thought of accosting two girls unless he saw they were really in need of help."

I laughed — I am afraid I laughed. I thought mother was so very innocent.

"I hope you thanked him for his trouble," added she. "Being the Squire's nephew, as it seems he was, I shouldn't be pleased to think you treated him as short as you sometimes treat strangers. You, Margaret, I mean," added mother, looking at me.

"Oh yes, we were very polite to him," said I. And then I grew very hot. Of course I knew I was bound to say that Captain Forrester had driven us home. I hoped mother would take it kindly, as she seemed well disposed towards him, but I did not feel perfectly sure.

"We asked him to come in, didn't we, Joyce?" added I, looking at her.

"Yes, we did," murmured my sister, bending very low over her plate.

"Asked him to come where?" asked mother.

"Why, here, to be sure," cried I, growing bolder. "He drove us home, you know."

Mother said nothing, for Deborah had

just brought in the pudding, and she was always very discreet before servants at meal-times. But she closed her lips in a way that I knew, and her face assumed an aggrieved kind of expression that she only put on to me: when Joyce was in the wrong, she always scolded her quite frankly. There was silence until Deborah had left the room. She went out with a smile on her face which always drove me into a frenzy, for it meant to say, "You are in for it, and serve you right;" and I thought it was taking advantage of her position in the family to notice any differences that occurred between mother and the rest of us.

When Deborah had gone out, shutting the door rather noisily, mother laid down her knife and fork. She did not look at me at all, she looked at Joyce. That was generally the way she punished me.

"You don't mean to say, Joyce, that you allowed a strange gentleman to get into the trap before all the townsfolk!" said she. "You're the eldest,—you ought to have known better."

I could not stand this. "It isn't Joyce's

fault," said I boldly; "I thought we were in luck's way when the gentleman offered to drive us. He knew the mare, and of course I felt that we were safe."

"It will be all over the place to-morrow," said mother, pathetically.

"Well, the gentleman is the Squire's nephew, and everybody knows what friends you are with the Squire," answered I provokingly.

"You might see that makes it all the worse," answered mother. "I don't know how ever I shall meet the Squire again. I'm ashamed to think my daughters should have behaved so unseemly. But the ideas of young women in these days pass me. Such notions wouldn't have gone down in my day. Young women were forced to mind themselves if they were to have a chance of a husband. Your father would never have looked at me if I had been one of that sort."

Father was in a brown study. I do not think he had paid much attention to the affair at all, but now he smiled as mother glanced across at him, seeming to expect some recognition. She repeated her last remark and then he said, bowing to her with old-fashioned gallantry: "I think I should have looked at you, Mary, whatever your shortcomings had been. You were too pretty to be passed over."

And he smiled again, as he never smiled at any one but mother,—the smile that, when it did come, lit up his face like a dash of broad sunshine upon a rugged moor.

"But mother's quite right, lassies," added he; "a woman must be modest and gentle, not self-seeking nor eager for homage, or she'll never have all the patience she need have to put up with a man's tempers."

He sighed, and the tears rose to my eyes. A word of disapproval from my father always hurt me to the quick, and I felt that in this case it was not wholly deserved, as, however mistaken I might have been, I had certainly not been self-seeking or eager for homage.

"I'm very sorry," said I, but I am afraid not at all humbly; "I didn't know I was doing anything so very dreadful. Anyhow it wasn't I who was afraid of the horse, and it wasn't for me that Captain Forrester took the reins."

This was quite true, but I had no business to have said it. I wished the words back as soon as they were spoken. Joyce blushed scarlet again, and mother looked at me for the first time. I felt that she was going to ask what I meant, but father interrupted her.

"There, there," said he, not testily, but as though to put an end to the discussion. "You should not have done it, because mother says so, and mother always knows best, but I daresay there's little harm done. A civil word hurts nobody, and as for the mare, you needn't drive her again."

So that was all that I had got for my pains. I opened my mouth to explain and to remonstrate, but father rose from the table and said grace, and I dared not pursue the subject further. For the matter of that, the look of pain in his face, as he moved across the room and sat down heavily in the chair, was quite enough to chase away my vexation against him. "Meg, just take these heavy things off for me, I'm weary," said he. I knelt down and unfastened the gaiters and unlaced the heavy boots, and brought him his slippers. He lay back with a sigh of relief.

"The walk round the farm has been too much for you, Laban," said mother, sitting down in the other high-backed chair near him.

"Let be, let be," muttered he.

"Nay, I can't let be, Laban," insisted mother. "I must look after your health, you know. I can see very well that it is too much for you seeing after the farm as it should be seen after. And that's why I don't think the Squire's notion is half a bad one."

I stopped with the spoons and forks in my hand that I was taking off the table. Father made that noise between his teeth again. I always knew it meant a storm brewing.

"Anyhow, I hope you won't bear him a grudge for what he thought fit to advise," mother went on. "He did it out of friendship, I'm sure. And the Squire's a wise man."

Father did not answer at first. He had risen and stood with his back to the fire.

His jaw was set, his eyes looked like black beads under the overhanging brows.

"Of course I know you'll say he just wants to get a job for his friend's son," continued mother. "And no doubt he mightn't have thought of it but for this turning up. But he wouldn't advise it if he didn't think it was for our good. The Squire has our interests at heart, I'm sure."

"Damn the Squire," said father at last, slowly and below his breath. Mother laid her hand on his arm.

"Hush, Laban, hush; not before the girls," said she in her gentle tones.

"Well, well, there," said he. "The Squire's a good man and an honest man, but I say neither he nor any one else has a right to come and teach a man what to do with his own."

"He doesn't do it because of any right," persisted mother. "He does it because he's afraid things don't work as well as they used to do, and because he's your friend."

"And what business has he to be afraid?" retorted father. "I say the land's my own, though I do pay him rent for it, and it's my business to be afraid. Does he think I shall be behind-hand with the rent? I've been punctual to a day these last twenty years. What more does he want, I should like to know?"

"Now, Laban, you know that isn't it," expostulated mother. "He knows he is safe enough for the rent, but he's afraid you ain't making money so fast as you might. And of course if you aren't, it's clear it's because you're not so strong to work as you were, and you haven't got a son of your own to look after things for you."

Mother sighed as she said this, but I am afraid I looked at her with angry not sympathetic eyes.

"The Squire takes a true interest in us all," repeated she for the third time, her voice trembling a little.

"Well, then, let him take his interest elsewhere this time, ma'am, that's all I've got to say," retorted father, in no way appeased. "If things were as they should be, there'd be no paying of rent to eat up a man's profits on the land, but what he made by the sweat of his brow would be his own for his old age, and for his children after him. And if we can only get what ought to belong to the nation by paying for it, then all I bargain for is—let those who get the money from me leave alone prying into how I get it together."

I had stood perfectly still all this time, with the spoons and forks in my hand, listening and wondering. Father's last speech I had scarcely given heed to. I had heard those opinions before, and they had become mere words in my ears. I was entirely engrossed with wondering what was the exact nature of the Squire's suggestion, and with horror at what I feared. I was not long left in doubt.

"Well, you make a great mistake in being angry with Squire Broderick, Laban, indeed you do," reiterated mother, shaking her head, and without paying any attention to his fiery speech. She never did pay any attention to such speeches. She always frankly said that she did not understand them. "If the Squire recommends this young Mr Trayton Harrod to you, it is because he knows him and thinks he would work with you, and not be at all like any common paid bailiff. I'm sure of that."

"Well, then, mother, all I can say is—it's nonsense,—that is what it is. It is nonsense. If a man is a paid bailiff, the more like one he is the better. And I don't think it is at all likely I shall ever take a paid bailiff to help me to manage Knellestone."

With that he strode to the door and opened it.

"Meg, will you please come to me in my study in a quarter of an hour," said he, turning to me as he went out. "There are a few things in the farm accounts that I think you might help me with."

CHAPTER VI.

I WENT into the sunlight and stood leaning upon the garden-hedge looking out over the glittering plain of snow to the glittering blue of the sea beyond. The whole scene was set with jewels of light, and even the grey fortress in the marsh seemed to awaken for once out of its sleep; but I was in no mood to laugh with the sunbeams, for my heart was beating with angry thoughts. A bailiff, a manager for Knellestone—and Knellestone that had been managed by nobody but its own masters for three hundred years! It was impossible! Why, the very earth would rise up and rebel! From where I stood I could see our meadows down on the marsh, our fields away on the hills towards the sunset, the pastures where our shepherds spent cold nights in huts at the lambing-time, the land where our oxen drew the plough and our labourers tilled the soil and harvested the ingatherings. Would the men and the beasts work for the manager as they worked for us? Would the land prosper for a stranger and a hireling, who would not care whether the cattle lived or died, whether the seasons were kind or cruel, whether the trees and the flowers flourished or pined away,—who would get his salary just the same though the frost nipped the new crops, though the wheat dried up for want of rain or rotted in the ear for lack of sun, though the cows cast their calves and the lambs died at the birth? How absurd, how ridiculous it was! Did it not show that it had been suggested by one who took no interest in the land, but who let it all out to others to care for! Of course this was some spendthrift younger son of a ruined gentleman's family, or some idiot who had failed at every other profession, and was to be sent here to ruin other people without having any responsibility of his own,—somebody to whom the Squire owed a duty or a favour. Perhaps a man who had never been on a farm in his life, maybe had not even lived in the country at all. In my childish anger I became utterly unreasonable, and gave vent in my solitude to any absurd expressions that occurred to me. I smile to myself as I remember the impotent rage of that afternoon. Indeed I think I hated the Squire most thoroughly that day. It was the idea, too, that I was being set at naught that added to my anger. Hitherto it was I who had transmitted father's orders to the men whenever he was laid by or busy; and as I have said before, he often trusted me to ride to the bank with money, and even to take stock of the goods before sales and fairs came on. Of course I know now that I was worse than useless to him. I was a clever girl enough, and dauntless in the matter of fatigue or trouble, but I was entirely ignorant of the hundred little details that make all the difference in matters of that kind, and pluck and coolness stood me in poor stead of experience. But at that time I was confident, and as I stood there looking at the brightness that I did not see, tears came into my eyes—tears of mortification that even the Squire should have considered me so perfectly useless that I could be set aside as though I did not exist. How often I had wished to be a boy! How heartily I wished it that afternoon! If I had been a boy there would never even have been a question of getting a paid manager to help father. I should have been a man by this time, nearly of age, and no one would have doubted that I was clever enough and strong enough to see after my own.

Father called from the window, and I went in. He was sitting by the table, surrounded by papers, his foot supported on a chair.

"Sit down, Meg," said he. "I want you to help me remember one or two things in the books that I don't quite understand,—I think you can."

He spoke quite cheerfully. I had been setting down things in the book while he had been ill, and paying the wages to the men, and it was quite natural he should want to see me about it. I sat down, and we went over the books item by item. We had had a very sound education though simple, quite as good as most girls have, and I had been considered more than usually smart at figures.

But that day I think I was dazed. I could not remember things; I could not tell why the books were not square; my wits were muddled on every point. Father was most patient, most kind. I think he must have seen that I was over-anxious,—but his kindness only made me more disgusted with myself; for I knew that that dreadful question was in his mind the whole time, as it was in mine. Whenever I told him anything that was not satisfactory in the conduct of affairs, or anything that had failed to turn out as he expected, I knew that it was in his mind although he did not think that I saw it.

"We can't expect old heads to grow on young shoulders," said he at last, patting mine gently, a thing most rare for him to do. "It takes many a long day to learn experience, my dear. And sometimes we don't do so much better with it than we did without it." He put the books away as he spoke, and leant back in his chair. "That'll do now, child," he added; "to-morrow I shall be able to see the men myself. I am well and hearty again now—thank the Lord—and a good bit of work will do me good."

"You mustn't begin too soon, father," said I, timidly; "you know the weather is very cold and treacherous yet."

"Oh, you women would keep a man indoors for ever for fear the wind should blow in his face," cried he, testily. "But there's an end to everything. When I'm ill you shall all do what you like with me, but when I'm well I mean to be my own master."

"But I shall still be able to help you, father, as I have done before—shan't I?" added I, still, singularly, without my accustomed self-confidence.

"Why, yes, child, of course," he replied. "And you and I will be able to get on yet awhile without a stranger's help, I'll warrant." It was the only allusion he had made to the horrible subject during the whole of our interview. It was the only allusion he made to it in my presence for many a long day. He rose from his chair as he spoke the last words, and walked across to the window.

The afternoon was beginning to sink, and the sun had paled in its splendour. The lights were grey now over the whiteness of the marsh, and the snow looked cold and cruel. Something made my heart sink, too, as I noticed how grey was father's face in the scrutinising light of the afternoon. I had not noticed before that he had really been ill. I left the room quickly, and went out again. The stinging March air struck a chill into my bones, and yet it was scarcely more than four o'clock. Two hours of daylight yet! How was it possible that any man but the strongest should work as a man must work whose farm should prosper? And was father really a strong man? I was sick with misgivings. What if, after all, the Squire were right? But I would not believe it. Father had had the gout; it was always the strongest men who had the gout.

I turned to go indoors. A laugh greeted my ears from the library. I passed before the window. Yes; it was father who was laughing as he shook hands with a man who had just entered the room. I looked. The man was a tall, blond, spare fellow, with a sanguine complexion, very marked features, small grey eyes, and a bald head. I knew him to be a Mr Hoad, father's solicitor in town. He was well dressed in a black suit and grey trousers. He was a very successful man for his time of life, people said. I knew that father liked him, and I was glad that father should have a visitor who cheered him to-day. But for my own part, I knew no one who filled me with such a peculiar antipathy. I could not bear the sight of the man. Yet he was a harmless kind of fellow, and very polite to ladies. Joyce often used to take me to task for my excessive dislike to him. If it was because I did not consider him on equal terms with us, from a social point of view—for I must confess I was ridiculously prejudiced on this score, and where I had learnt such nonsense I do not know—then the shipowners and other people of that class to whom I could give "good day" in town were much less so. But I could not have told why I disliked him so particularly; I could not have told why I wondered that father could have any dealings with him, —why I was always on the watch for something that should prove that I was in the right in my instinct. And somehow his appearance on this particular evening affected me even more uncomfortably than usual, and

I felt that I could not go in and see him—perhaps even have to discuss the very subject that was weighing on my mind—when I wanted to be alone to nurse my own mortification, and lull my fears to rest by myself. I crept into the hall quietly and fetched a cloak and hood, and then, running round to the yard, I called the St Bernard. He came, leaping and jumping upon me, this friend with whom I was always in tune. I opened the gate gently, and together we went out upon the road.

I think Taff and I must have walked three miles. The roads were stiff and slippery, the air was like a knife; but I did not care. The quick movement and the solitude and the quiet of the coming night soothed me. We got up upon the downs where lonely homesteads stud the country here and there, and came back again along the cliffs that crown the marshland. There I stood a long while face to face with the quiet world upon which the moon had now risen in the deep blue of a twilight sky. It looked down upon the wide white marsh upon whose frozen bosom grey vapours floated lightly;

it looked down upon the dark town that rose yonder so sombre and distinct out of the mystery of the landscape; the channel that flows to the sea lay cold and blue and motionless at the foot of the hill, like a sheet of steel. It made me shudder. There was not a ripple upon its deathly breast. The snow around was far more tender. For the first time in my life I felt the sadness of the world; I realised that there was something in it which I could not understand; I remembered that there was such a thing as death.

CHAPTER VII.

I DID not escape Mr Hoad by my walk. He had stayed to tea. I do not think that he was a favourite of mother's, but she always made a great point of welcoming all father's friends to the house, and I saw that she had welcomed him to-night. He sat in the place of honour beside her, and there were sundry alterations on the tea-table, and a pot of special marmalade in the middle.

It was very late when I came in. I took off my things in the hall and went in without smoothing my hair. I thought I should have been in disgrace for coming in late, and for having my hair in disorder when a guest was present; but mother had forgotten her displeasure, and smiled as she pushed my cup towards me. She never made any allusion to bygone differences; her anger never lasted long.

The mood that I had brought with me from without was still upon me, and when I saw that father's face had lost its grey pallor, that his eyes shone with their usual fire, and that his voice was strong and healthy, I sighed a sigh of relief and told myself that I was a fool, and that Mr Hoad must really be a good fellow if he could so soon chase away the gloom from my parent's brow.

"Your husband looks wonderfully well again, Mrs Maliphant," he was saying; "it's quite surprising how soon he has pulled round. When I met the doctor the other day driving from town and stopped to ask after him, he said it would be weeks before he could be about again. But he has got a splendid constitution — must have. Not that I would wish to detract from your powers of nursing. We all have heard how wonderful they are."

Mr Hoad smiled at mother, but she did not smile back again. There were people whom she kept at arm's length, even though carefully civil to them. I don't suppose she knew this, for she was a shy woman, but I recollect it well.

"We can all nurse those we are fond of," she said. "I'm sure I'm very pleased to think you should find Mr Maliphant looking better."

"Better! Nonsense!" exclaimed father. "I'm as well as I ever was in my life. Don't let's hear any more about that, wife, there's a dear soul."

"Nay, you shall hear no more about it than need be from me, Laban, I can promise you that," smiled mother, pouring out the tea, while Joyce, from the opposite side of the table, where she was cutting up the seed-cake that she had made with her own hands the day before, asked the guest after his two daughters.

"They are very busy," answered Mr Hoad. "A large acquaintance, you know,—it involves a great deal of calling. I'm afraid they have been remiss here."

"Oh, pray, don't mention such a thing, Mr Hoad," exclaimed mother hastily. "We don't pay calls ourselves. We are plain folk, and don't hold with fashionable ways."

Mr Hoad smiled rather uncomfortably.

"And we have not much to amuse them

with," I put in. "We do nothing that young ladies do."

I saw mother purse up her lips at this, and I was vexed that I had said it; but father laughed, and said: "No, Hoad, my girls are simple farmer's daughters, and have learnt more about gardening and housekeeping than they have about French and piano-playing, though Meg can sing a ballad when she chooses as well as I want to hear it."

I declared that my voice was nothing to Miss Hoad's; and Joyce, always gracious, looked across to Mr Hoad and said: "I wonder whether Miss Jessie would sing something for us at our village concert?"

"I'll ask her," said Mr Hoad, a little diffidently. "I'm never sure about my daughters' engagements. They have so many engagements."

"We shall be very pleased to see them here any afternoon for a practice, shan't we mother?" added Joyce.

"The young ladies will always be welcome," replied mother, a little stiffly; and I hastened to add, I fear less graciously:

"But pray don't let them break any engagements for us."

Mr Hoad smiled again, and then father turned to him and they took up the thread of their own talk where they had left it.

"You certainly ought to know that young fellow I was speaking of," Mr Hoad began. "I was struck with him at once. A wonderful gift of expressing himself, and just that kind of way with him that always wins people, one can't explain it. Handsome, too, and full of enthusiasm."

"Enthusiasm don't always carry weight," objected father. "It's rather apt to fly too high."

"Bound to fly high when you have got to get over the heads of other folks," laughed Mr Hoad.

Father looked annoyed. "I wasn't joking, I wasn't joking," said he. "If men want to go in for great work, they can't afford to take it lightly." And then he added with one of his quick looks, "But don't misunderstand me, Hoad. Enthusiasm of the right kind never takes things lightly. It's the only sort of stuff that wins great battles, because it has plenty of courage and don't know the meaning of failure. Only, there's such lots of stuff that's called enthusiasm and is nothing but gas. I should like to see this young man and judge for myself. God forbid I should think youth a stumbling-block. Youth is the time for doing as well as for dreaming."

Father sighed, and though I could not tell why at the time, I can guess now that it was from the recollection of that friend of his who must have been the type of youthful enthusiasm thus to have left his memory and the strength of his convictions so many years in the heart of another.

"Well, you can see him easily enough," said Mr Hoad. "He's staying in your village, I believe. He's a nephew of Squire Broderick's."

"What! Captain Forrester?" cried I.

"Ah, you know him of course, Miss Maliphant. Trust the young ladies for finding out the handsome men," said Mr Hoad, turning to me with his most irritating expression of gallantry. I bit my lips with annoyance at having opened my mouth to the man, especially as he glanced across at

Joyce with a horribly knowing look, at which of course she blushed, making me very angry.

"I fancy the Squire and he don't get on so extra well together," said Mr Hoad. "Squire don't like the look of the lad that'll step into his shoes, if he don't make haste and marry and have a son of his own, I suppose."

"I should think this smart captain had best not reckon too much on the property," said mother stiffly, up in arms at once for her favourite. "The Squire's young enough yet to marry and have a dozen sons."

"Yes, yes, ma'am, only joking, only joking," declared Mr Hoad. "I shouldn't think the lad gave the property a thought."

"If he's the kind of man you say, he can't possibly care about property," said I, glibly, talking of what I could not understand. Father smiled — but smiled kindly at me. Mr Hoad laughed outright and made me furious.

"I see you're up in all the party phrases, young lady," said he.

"How did you come to know the young

man, Hoad?" asked father, without giving me time to reply. "You seem to have become friends in a very short time."

"He came to me on a matter of business," repeated Hoad evasively. "I fancy he's pretty hard up. Only got his captain's pay and a little private property, on his father's side, I suppose, and no doubt gives more than he can spare to these societies and things."

Father was silent. Probably he knew, what I had no notion of, that there was another branch to Mr Hoad's profession besides that of a solicitor. Evidently he did not like to be reminded of the fact, for he knitted his brow and let his jaw fall, as he always did when annoyed.

"I don't know how we came to talk politics," Hoad went on, "but we did, and I thought to myself, 'why, here's just the man for Maliphant.' I never knew any one else go as far as you do; but this young fellow—why, he nearly beat you, 'pon my soul he did!"

"Politics!" echoed father, frowning more unmistakably than ever; "what have they got to do with the matter?"

"Come, now, Maliphant, you're not going to keep that farce up for ever," cried Mr Hoad, in his most intimate and good-natured fashion. Oh, how I resented it when he would treat father as though he were on perfect equality with him! For my father's daughter I was intolerant; but then Mr Hoad patronised, and patronising was not necessary in order to be consistent.

"What do you mean?" asked father.

"It was all very well for you to swear you would have nothing to do with us before," continued Mr Hoad. "You did not think we should ever get hold of a man who looked at things as you do. But now we have. And if you really have the Radical cause at heart, as you say, you will be able to get him in for the county. He has got everything in his favour—good name, good presence, good breeding. Those are the men to run your notions; not your measly, workaday fellows,—they have no influence with the masses."

Father rose from the table. His eyebrows nearly met in their overhanging shagginess, and his eyes were small and brilliant.

"I don't think I understand you, Hoad," said he. "We seem to be at cross purposes. Do you mean to say that this young man wants to get into Parliament?"

"Oh, no plans, no plans whatever, I should say," said Hoad. "He merely asked me who was going to contest the Tory seat, and when I asked him if he was a Radical, he aired a few sentiments which, as I tell you, are quite in your line. But I should think we might easily persuade him—he seemed so very eager. If you would back our man, Maliphant, we should be safe whoever he was, I do believe," added the solicitor, emphatically. "He has a really wonderful influence with the working classes, that husband of yours, ma'am," he finished up, turning to mother.

"Yes," said she proudly; "Laban's a fine orator. When I heard him speak at the meeting the other day, he fairly took my breath away, that he did."

Mother looked up at father with a pleased smile, for she loved to hear him praised, but for my own part I knew very well that he was in no mood for pleasant speeches.

"I have always told you, Hoad, that it's no part of my scheme to go in for politics," said he, in a low voice, but very decisively. "I see no reason to change my mind."

"Well, my dear fellow, but that's absurd," answered Mr Hoad, still in that provokingly friendly fashion. "How ever do you expect to get what you want?"

"Not through Parliament, anyhow," said father, laconically. "I never heard of any Act of Parliament that gave bread to the poor out of the waste of the rich. I'll wait to support Parliament till I see one of the law-makers there lift up a finger to right the poor miserable children who swarm and starve in the London streets, and whose little faces grow mean and sharp with the learning to cheat those who cheat them of their daily bread."

I can see him now, his lip trembling, his eye bright, his hands clenched. It was the cry with which he ended every discourse: this tender pity for the many children who must needs hunger while others waste, who must needs learn sin while others are shielded from even knowing that there is such a thing: those innocent sinners, outcasts from good, patient because hopeless, yet often enough incurably happy even in the very centre of evil, — they were always in his heart. It was his most cherished hope in some way to succour them, by some means to bring the horror of their helplessness home to the hearts of those who had happy children of their own.

I held my face down that no one should see my tears, and I knew that father took out his big coloured pocket-handkerchief and blew his nose very hard. Mr Hoad, however, was not so easily affected.

"Ah! you were right, Mrs Maliphant," said he, in a loud, emphatic voice. "Your husband would make a very fine orator. All the more reason it's a sin and a shame he should hide his talents under a bushel. Now, don't you agree with me?"

"Oh, Laban knows best what he has got to do," answered mother. "I think it's a great pity for women to mix themselves up in these matters. They have plenty to do attending to the practical affairs of life."

Mr Hoad burst into a loud fit of laughter. "Ah, you've got a clever wife, Maliphant," cried he. "She's put her finger upon the weak joint in your armour! Yes, that's it, my boy. They're fine sentiments, but they aren't practical; they won't wash. But you would soon see, when you really got into the thing, that the best way to make the first step towards what you want, is not to ask for the whole lot at once. The thin edge of the wedge—that's the art. And I should be inclined to think this young fellow was not wanting in tact."

"Anyhow," answered father quietly, "if Squire Broderick's nephew were minded to oppose the Tory candidate for this county, I should certainly not wish, as Squire Broderick's old friend, to support him in his venture."

"Ah, you're very scrupulous, Maliphant," laughed Mr Hoad. But then, seeing his mistake, he added quickly: "Quite right, perfectly right of course, and I don't suppose the young man has any intention of doing anything of the kind."

"No doubt it was rather that the wish

was father to the thought in you, Hoad," answered father frankly.

"Ah, well, you may be as obstinate as you like, Maliphant," said the solicitor, trying to take father's good-tempered effort as a cue for jocoseness, "but we can get on very well without you if the young ladies will only give us their kind support. I hope you won't be such an old curmudgeon as to forbid that; and I hope," added he, turning to Joyce with that sugary smile of his, "that the young ladies will not withdraw their patronage if, after all, a less handsome man than Captain Forrester should be our Radical candidate."

"Oh, thank you," said Joyce, blushing furiously, and looking up with distressed blue eyes; "indeed we scarcely know Captain Forrester at all. We couldn't possibly be of any use to you."

"Of course not," cried I. "Whoever were the candidate, we should not canvass. We never canvass. We are not politicians."

I wonder that nobody smiled, but nobody did. Father was too busy with his thoughts, and perhaps Mr Hoad was too much astonished. But as though to cover my priggishness, Joyce said sweetly, when Mr Hoad rose to go, " You won't forget the concert, will you ? And, please, will you tell Miss Bessie that I shall be very glad to do what I can to help her with her bazaar work."

He promised to remember both messages, and shook hands with her in a kind of lingering way, which I remember was a manner he always had towards a pretty girl. I thought mother took leave of him a little shortly. Father alone accompanied him out into the hall, and saw him into the smart little gig that came round from the stable to pick him up. I went to the pantry for the tray to clear the tea things. When I came back again into the parlour Joyce had gone upstairs, and father and mother were alone. I do not know why it was, but as soon as I came in I felt sure that the discussion with Hoad, eager as it had been at the time, was not occupying father's mind. I felt sure that mother had alluded to that more important matter hotly spoken of after the Squire's visit. She was standing by the fire, and father held her hand in his. He asked me to bring a lamp into his study, and went out. I glanced at mother.

"What does father want to go to work for so late?" said I. "Why don't he sit and smoke his pipe as usual?"

Mother did not answer: her back was turned towards me, but there was something in its expression which made me feel sure that she was crying.

"But he seems much better to-night, mother," I added, coming up behind her; "he was quite himself over that argument."

"Yes, dear, yes, he can always wake up over those things," answered she, and sure enough there was a tremble in her voice, and every trace of the dignity that she had used towards me since the scene at the dinner-table had entirely disappeared.

"Dear mother, why do you fret?" said I softly. "I'm sure there's no need."

"No, no, of course there's no need," she repeated. "But, Margaret," added she, hurriedly, as though she were half ashamed of what she were saying, "if he could be brought to see that plan of the Squire's in a better light, I'm sure it would be a good thing. I don't think his heart has ever been in farm-work, and I can't a-bear to see him working so hard now he is old. It would have been different you see if—if little John had lived."

I kissed her silently. The innocent slight to my own capacities, which had so occupied my mind an hour ago, passed unnoticed by me. And as father that night at family prayers rolled forth in his sonorous voice the beautiful language of the Psalms, the words, " He hath respect unto the lowly, but the proud he knoweth afar off," sank into my heart, and I thought that I should never again want to set myself up above my betters.

CHAPTER VIII.

I LAY awake quite half an hour that night, and I made up my mind—just as seriously as though my feelings were likely to prove an important influence—that I would in no way try to bias my father in his decision about taking a bailiff. But real as was my trouble about this matter that to me was so mighty, it was all put to flight the next morning by an occurrence of more personal and immediate interest. Such is the blessed elasticity of youth. The occurrence was one which not only brought the remembrance of Captain Forrester, and my romantic dreams for Joyce, once more vividly to my mind, but it also gave no small promise of enjoyment to myself; it consisted in the sudden appearance of a groom from the Manor, who delivered into my hands a note for mother.

It was morning when he came: mother was still in the kitchen with Deborah, and Joyce and I had not finished making our beds and dusting our room. But I do not think there was any delay in the answering of that door-bell. I remember how cross I was when mother would insist on finishing all her business before she opened the note : she went into the poultry-yard and decided what chickens and what ducks should be killed for the week's dinners, she went into the dairy to look at the cream, she even went up herself into the loft to get apples before she would go and find her spectacles in the parlour. And yet any one could have imagined that a note from the Squire meant something very important. And so indeed it did. It contained a formal invitation to a grand ball, to be given at the Manor house. The card did not say a "grand" ball, but of course we knew that it would be a grand ball. We were fairly dazed with excitement. Actually a ball in our quiet little village! Such a thing had not been known since I had been grown up, and I had not even heard of its having occurred since the days when young Mrs Broderick had come to the Manor as a bride. Of course we had been to dances in town once or twice—once to the Hoads', and once to a county ball, got up at the White Hart Inn, but I think these were really the only two occasions on which I had danced anywhere out of the dancing academy. Joyce, being a little older, could count about three more such exciting moments in her life. The card was passed round from hand to hand, and then stuck up on the mantel-shelf in front of the clock, as though there were any danger that any of the family would be likely to forget on what day and at what hour Squire Broderick had invited us to "dancing" at the Manor.

"I wonder what has made the Squire give a ball now?" said mother. "I suppose it's the prospect of the elections. He thinks he owes it to the county."

"Why on earth should he owe the county a ball because of the elections!" cried I. "He is not going to stand, and I don't think he can suppose that a ball would be likely to do the Farnham interests much good, if that's the only man they have got to put forward on the Conservative side."

"I don't think it's a young girl's business to talk in that flippant way, Margaret," said the mother. Father was not present just then. "I don't think it's becoming in young folk to talk about matters they can't possibly understand."

I was nettled at this, but I did not dare to answer mother back.

"You never heard your father talk like that of Mr Farnham, I'm sure," added mother. "He likes him a great deal better than he does Mr Thorne, although Mr Thorne is a Radical."

"Well, I should think so! Mr Thorne is a capitalist, and father doesn't think that men who have made such large fortunes in business ought to exist," cried I boldly, applying a theory to an individual as I thought I had been taught. "It is no use his being a Radical, nor giving money to the poor, because he oughtn't to have the money. It's dreadful to think of his having bought a beautiful old place like the Priory with money that he has ground out of his work-people. No, nobody will ever like Mr Thorne in the neighbourhood."

"I know Squire and he don't hold together at all," answered mother. "Though they do say Mr Thorne bought the property through that handsome young spark of a nephew of the Squire's. The families were acquainted up North."

"Who told you that, mother?" asked I quickly.

"Miss Farnham said so when she called yesterday," replied mother. "And she said it was Mr Thorne was going to contest the seat with her brother, so I don't know how Mr Hoad could have come suggesting that young captain to your father as he did yesterday. A rich man like the manufacturer would be sure to have much more chance."

I was silent. I was a little out of my depth. "I don't believe Mr Hoad knew anything at all about it," I said. "How could a man be going to contest a seat against the candidate that his own uncle was backing? It's ridiculous. Mr Hoad has always got something to say."

"Margaret, you really shouldn't allow yourself to pass so many opinions on folk," repeated mother. "First Mr Farnham, and then Mr Thorne, and now Mr Hoad. It's not pretty in young women."

"Very well, mother, I won't do it again," said I, merrily. "At all events, Parliament doesn't matter much—father says so; and anyhow Squire's going to give us a ball, and nothing can matter so much as that."

Nothing did matter half so much to us three just then, it is true. Mother was just as much excited as we were, and we all fell to discussing the fashions with just as much eagerness, if not as much knowledge, as if we had been London born and bred.

"You must look over your clothes and see you have got everything neat. Joyce, I suppose you will wear your white embroidered 'India,'" said the mother. And from that it was a very natural step to go and look at the white muslin, and at the other clothes that our simple wardrobes boasted, so that we spent every bit of that morning that was not taken up with urgent household duties, in turning over frocks and laces and ribbons, and determining what we should wear, and what wanted washing before we did wear it. Yes, I think I thought of my dress that day for the first time in my life. There was no need to think of Joyce's, because she was sure to be admired; but if there was any chance of my looking well, it could only be because of some happy thought with regard to my costume; and so when mother suggested that she should give me her lovely old sea-green shot silk to be made up for the occasion, my heart leapt for joy. I was very much excited. For Joyce, because I had quite made up my mind that it was Captain Forrester who had persuaded the Squire to give this ball; and for myself, because it was really a great event in the life of any girl, and I was passionately fond of dancing. I spent the afternoon washing my old lace ruffles, and pulling them out tenderly before the fire, and all the time I was humming waltz tunes, and wondering who would dance with me, and picturing Joyce to myself whirling round in the arms of Captain Forrester. I thought of Joyce and her lover so much that it was scarcely a surprise to me when, just as the light was beginning to fade and tea-time was near, I heard a sharp ring at the front door, and running to the back passage window with my lace in my hand, I saw that Squire Broderick was standing in the porch, and with him his nephew, Captain Forrester. I heard Joyce fly through the hall to the kitchen. I think she must have seen the two gentlemen pass down the road, and then she ran back again into the parlour, and Deborah went to the door.

"Mrs Maliphant at home?" said the Squire's cheery voice; and scarcely waiting for a reply, he strode through to the front room.

I threw down my lace, turned down my sleeves, and without any more attention to my toilet I ran down-stairs. Mother had gone to do some little errands in the village and had not come in: Joyce stood alone with the visitors. She had her plain darkblue everyday gown on, but the soft little frills at her throat and wrists were clean. I remember thinking how fortunate it was that they were clean. She was standing in the window with Captain Forrester, who was admiring our view over the marsh.

"It's a most beautiful country," said he. And his eyes wandered from the plain without that the shades of evening were slowly darkening, to the face at his side that shone so fair against the little frilled muslin curtain which she held aside with her hand.

The Squire sat at the table; he had taken up the morning paper, and I supposed that the frown on his face was summoned there by something that he read in the columns of this, the Liberal journal. Captain Forrester left Joyce and came towards me as soon as I entered the room.

"Miss Maliphant, I am delighted to meet you again," said he, with his pleasant polished manner that had the art of never making one feel that he was saying a thing merely to be agreeable. "After our little adventure of the other day, I felt that it was impossible for me to leave the neighbourhood without trying to make our acquaintance fast."

"Oh, are you leaving the neighbourhood?" said I,—I am afraid a little too anxiously.

"Well, not just yet," smiled Captain Forrester. "I think I shall stay till over the ball."

"Nonsense, Frank," said the Squire, rising and pushing the paper away from him. "Of course you will stay over the ball." Then turning to me, he said merrily, "No difficulty about you young ladies coming, I hope?"

"I don't know, Mr Broderick," answered I. "You must wait and ask mother. It's a very grand affair for two such simple girls as Joyce and me."

"Oh, Margaret, I think we shall be allowed to go," put in Joyce in her gentle, matter-of-fact voice. "You know we went to a very late ball last Christmas in town."

Considering that we had been sitting over frocks all the morning, this would have been nonsense, excepting that Joyce never could see a joke.

"I think I shall have to take Mrs Maliphant in hand myself if she makes any objection," said the Squire, "for we certainly can't spare you and your sister."

Joyce blushed, and Captain Forrester

turned to her and was going to say something which I think would have been complimentary, when father entered the room. He had his rough, brown, ill-cut suit on, and his blue handkerchief twisted twice round his neck and tied loosely in front, and did not look at all the same kind of man as the two in front of him. I noticed it for the first time that evening. I was not at all ashamed of it. If I had been questioned, I should have said that I was very proud of it, but I just noticed it, and I wondered if Captain Forrester noticed it too. It certainly was very odd that it never should have occurred to me before, that this lover whom I had picked out for Joyce belonged to the very same class as the Squire, whom I thought was so unsuitable to her. I suppose it was because Captain Forrester was not a landed proprietor, and that any man who belonged to the noble career of soldiering atoned for his birth by his profession.

"How are you, Maliphant?" said the Squire, grasping him by the hand as though there had been no such thing as any uncomfortable parting between them. " I'm glad to see you are none the worse for this cursed east wind. It's enough to upset many a younger and stronger man."

Father had taken the proffered hand, but not very cordially. I am not sure that he ever shook hands very cordially with people; perhaps it was partly owing to the stiffness in his fingers, but I believe that he regarded it as a useless formality. I imagine this because I, too, have always had a dislike to kissings and hand-shakings, when a simple "good-day" seemed to me to serve the purpose well enough.

"Pooh!" said father, in answer to the Squire's remark. "A man who has his work out-doors all the year round, Squire Broderick, needs must take little account whether the wind be in the east or the south, except as how it'll affect his crops and his flock."

The Squire took no notice of this speech. It was so very evident that it was spoken with a view to the vexed question.

"I've brought my nephew round," said he, and Captain Forrester left Joyce's side as he said it, and came forward with his pleasant smile and just the proper amount of deference added to his usual charming manner. "He wanted to see the Grange," added the Squire, again with that frown upon his brow that I could not understand, but which no doubt proceeded, as he had affirmed, from the effect of the east wind upon his temper.

"I'm very glad to see you, sir," said father shortly. "I hear you rendered my daughters some assistance the other day."

Captain Forrester smiled. "It could scarcely be called assistance," he said. "Your daughter"—and he looked at me to distinguish me from Joyce—"would have been capable of driving the horse, I am sure."

"Oh, I understood the mare reared," answered father.

"Well, she is not a good horse for a lady to drive," allowed Captain Forrester, as though the confession were wrung from him; and I wondered how he guessed that it annoyed me to be thought incapable of managing the mare. "But some women drive as well as any man."

The Squire took up the paper again. I did not think it was good manners of him.

"What a splendid view you have from this house," continued Captain Forrester. "I think it's much finer than from our place."

The Squire's shoulders moved with an impatient movement. The article he was reading must decidedly have annoyed him.

"Yes," answered Joyce; "but you should come and see it in summer or in autumn. It's very bleak now. The spring is so late this year."

"Ay; I don't remember a snowfall in March these five years," said father.

"But it has a beautiful effect on this plain," continued the young man, moving away into the window again. And then turning round to Joyce, he added, "Do you sketch, Miss Maliphant?"

"No, no," answered father for her. "We have no time for such things. We have all of us plenty to do without any accomplishments."

"Miss Margaret can sing 'Robin Adair,'" put in the Squire, "as well as I want to hear it, accomplishments or not."

"Indeed," said Captain Forrester, with a

show of interest. "I hope she will sing it to me some day."

He said it with a certain air of patronage, which I found afterwards came from his own excellent knowledge of music.

"Are you fond of singing?" said I, simply. I was too much of a country girl to think of denying the charge. I was very fond of good music; it was second nature to me, inherited, I suppose, from some forgotten ancester, and picking out tunes on the old piano was the only thing that ever kept me willingly indoors. Father delighted in my simple singing of simple ditties, and so did the Squire. I had grown used to thinking it was a talent in me, my only one, and I was not ashamed of owning up to it. "I'll sing it to you now if you like."

"That's very kind of you," said the young man, with a little smile. And I sat down and sang the old tune through. I remember that, for the first time in my life, I was really nervous. Captain Forrester stood by the piano. He was very kind; I don't know that any one had ever said so much to me about my voice before, but in spite of it all I knew for the first time that I knew nothing. I felt angrily ashamed when Joyce, in reply to pressing questions about her musical capacity, answered that I had all the talent, and began telling of the village concerts that I was wont to get up for the poor people, and of how there was one next week, when he must go and hear me sing.

"Certainly I will," he answered, pleasantly, "and do anything I can to help you. I have had some practice at that kind of thing."

"Why don't you say you are a regular professional at it, Frank?" put in the Squire, I fancied a little crossly. "He's always getting up village concerts—a regular godsend at that kind of thing."

Frank laughed, and said he hoped we would employ him after such a character, and then he asked what was our programme. Joyce told him. I was going to sing, and Miss Hoad was going to sing—and she sang beautifully, for she had learned in London—and then I would sing with the blacksmith, and Miss Thorne would play with the grocer on the cornet, and glees and comic songs would fill up the remainder. The smile upon Captain Forrester's face clouded just a little at the mention of Miss Thorne.

"Miss Thorne is not very proficient on the piano," said he. "Have you already asked her to perform?"

"Do you know Miss Thorne?" asked Joyce, surprised.

"Yes," answered the Captain; "she lived in the village where I was brought up as a boy—not far from Manchester. Her father was a great manufacturer, you know."

"Yes; we know that well enough." And I glanced uneasily at father; for if he knew that this young fellow was a friend of the Thornes, I was afraid it would set him against him. Luckily, he was busy talking to the Squire.

"She's a very nice girl," said Joyce, kindly, wanting to be agreeable, although indeed we knew no more of Mary Thorne than shaking hands with her coming out of church on a Sunday afternoon.

"Charming," acquiesced the Captain; "but she's not a good musician, and I shouldn't ask her to perform unless you're obliged to."

We said we were not obliged to; but Joyce said she wouldn't like to do anything unkind, and she was afraid Mary Thorne wanted to be asked to perform. And then they two retired into the window again, discussing the concert and the view, and I soon saw proudly that they were talking as though they had known one another for years. It generally took a long while for any one to get through the first ice with Joyce, but this man had an easy way with him; he was so sympathetic in his personality,—so kind and frank and natural.

"That's a most ridiculous article in the 'Herald,'" said the Squire to father. "I wonder Blair can put in such stuff. He's a sensible man."

"I wonder you'll admit even that, Squire," answered father, with a little laugh. The paper, I need not say, was the Liberal organ.

"Oh, well," smiled the other, "I can see the good in a man though I don't agree with him. But I think *that*"—pointing to the print—"is beneath contempt."

"I don't hold with it myself," answered father; "the man has got no pluck."

"Oh no, of course—doesn't go far enough for you, Maliphant," laughed the Squire; and at that moment mother came in, or I do not know what father would have answered. She came in slowly, and stood a moment in the doorway looking round upon us all. Joyce blushed scarlet, and came forward out of the recess. The Squire rose and hastened towards her.

"We have been invading your house while you have been away, Mrs Maliphant," said he. "That wasn't polite, was it? But you'll forgive me, I know."

Mother's eyes scarcely rested on him; they travelled past him to Captain Forrester, who stood in the window.

"My nephew, Frank Forrester," said the Squire, hastily following her look. The Captain advanced and bowed to mother. He could do nothing more, for she did not hold out her hand.

"I am very glad to see any friend of yours, Squire," said she. And then she turned away from him, and unfastened her cloak, which I took from her and hung up in the hall.

"Joyce, lay the cloth," said she. "We'll have tea at once." I left the room with sister.

"Never mind," whispered I outside, as we fetched the pretty white egg-shell cups that always came out when we had any company; "mother doesn't mean to be queer. She's just a little cold now, because she wants Captain Forrester to understand it wasn't with her leave we let him drive us home. But she isn't really cross."

"Cross! Oh, Margaret, no—of course not," echoed Joyce. She was taking down a plate from under a pile of cups, and said no more at the moment. I was ashamed and half vexed. That was the worst of Joyce. Sometimes she would reprove one when one was actually fighting her battles.

"Of course we ought not to have done it," continued she, setting the cups in order on the tray. "I felt it at the time."

"Then, why in the world didn't you say so?" cried I.

"I didn't know how to say so,—you scarcely gave me a chance," answered she. "Of course I know you did it because I was so stupidly frightened, but it makes me rather uncomfortable now."

"Oh, I thought you seemed to get on very well with Captain Forrester just now," said I huffily, kneeling down to reach the cake on the bottom shelf. "You seemed quite civil to him, and you didn't look uncomfortable."

"Didn't I? I'm glad," answered Joyce simply. "Of course one wants to be civil to the Squire's friends in father's house. And I do think he is a very polite gentleman."

She took up the tray and moved on into the parlour, and I went across into the kitchen to fetch the urn. I had never been envious of Joyce's beauty up to the present time. Nothing had happened to make me so, and I was fully occupied in being proud of it. But if her beauty was of such little account to her that she had not even been pleased by this handsome man's admiration of it,—well, I thought I could have made better use of it.

When I went into the parlour again the groups were all changed. Father stood by the fire, and the Squire had risen. Father had his hands crossed behind his back and his sarcastic expression on, and the Squire was talking loudly. Joyce was laying the cloth, and mother stood by the window where sister had stood before; Captain Forrester was talking to her as if he had never cared to do anything else. I could not hear what they were saying, the Squire's voice was too loud; but I could see that mother was quite civil.

"I never liked that man Hoad," the Squire was saying, and I felt a throb of satisfaction as I heard him. "I don't believe he's straightforward. Do anything for money, that's my feeling."

"He's a friend of mine," said father stiffly.

"Oh, well of course if he's a friend of yours, well and good," answered Mr Broderick shortly. "You probably know him better that I do. But I don't like him. I should never be able to trust him."

"Perhaps that is because you do not know him," suggested father.

"No doubt, no doubt," answered the Squire.

"I hear he has turned Radical now," added he, coming to the real core of the grievance. "He used to call himself a Liberal, but now I hear he calls himself a Radical, and is going to put up some Radical candidate to oppose us."

"Yes, I know," answered father, too honest to deny the charge.

"Oh, do you know who it is?" asked the Squire sharply

"No, I don't," answered father in the same way.

The Squire paused a moment; then he said, unable to keep it in, "Are you going to support him too?"

The colour went out of father's face: I knew he was angry.

"Well, Mr Broderick, I don't know what sort of a candidate it'll be," said he in a provoking manner. "There's Radicals and Radicals."

The Squire smacked his boot with his walking-stick and did not answer. Captain Forrester came forward, for mother had gone to the table to make the tea.

"Did I hear you say that you were a Radical, Mr Maliphant?" asked the young man, looking at father.

"I am not a Tory," answered father, without looking up. I thought his tone was cruelly curt.

"Well, I am a Socialist," answered Frank Forrester, with an air that would have been defiant had it not been too pleasant-spoken. Father smiled. The words must have provoked that—would have provoked more if the speaker had not been so good-tempered.

"Ah, I know what you young fellows mean by a Socialist," he murmured.

"I should say I went about as far as most men in England," said Frank, looking at him in that open-eyed fixed way that he used towards men as well as towards women.

"I should say that you went further than you can see," said the Squire laconically.

Frank laughed good-humouredly. "Ah, I refuse to quarrel with you, uncle," said he, taking hold of the Squire's arm in a friendly fashion. It was said as though he would imply that he could quarrel with other people when he liked, but his look belied his words.

"If you will let me, I'll come in and have a chat one of these days, Mr Maliphant," continued he. "When uncle is not by, you know." He said the words as though he felt sure that his request would be granted, and yet with his confidence there was a graceful deference to the elder man which was very fascinating. Why did father look at him as he did? Did he feel something that I felt? And what was it that I felt? I do not know.

"I am a busy man and haven't much time for talk, sir, but you're welcome when you like to call," answered father civilly, not warmly.

The Squire had sat down again while his nephew and father were exchanging these few words. He crossed one knee over the other and sat there striking his foot with his hand—a provoking habit that he had when he was trying to control his temper.

"There'll be a nice pair of you," said he, trying to turn the matter off into a joke. "It's a pity, Frank, that you have no vote to help Mr Maliphant's candidate with."

"I don't know that any so-called Radical

candidate would or could do much in Parliament to help the questions that I have at heart," said Captain Forrester. "As Mr Maliphant justly observed, there are Radicals and Radicals, and the political Radical has very little in common with those who consider merely social problems."

Father did look up now, and his eyes shone as I had seen them shine when he was talking to the working men; for though I had not often heard him—the chief of his discourses being given in the village club—I had once been to a large meeting in town where he had been the chief speaker.

"One never knows where to have any of you fellows," laughed the Squire, rather uncomfortably. "You always led me to believe, Maliphant, that you would have nothing to do with political party spirit. You always said that no party yet invented would advance the interests of the people in a genuine fashion; and now, as soon as a Radical candidate appears, you talk of supporting him."

"I'm not aware that I talked of supporting him," said father.

"But you won't return a Radical," continued the Squire, not hearing the remark. "The country isn't ripe for that sort of thing yet, whatever you may think it will be. You're very influential, I know. And if you're not with us, as I once hoped you might be, you'll be a big weight against us. But with all your influence, you won't return a Radical. The Tories are too strong; they're much stronger than they were last election, and then Sethurst was an old-fashioned Liberal and a well-known man in the county besides. You won't return a Radical. I don't believe there's a county in England would return what you would call a Radical, and certainly not ours."

"I don't believe there is," said father quietly.

"Then why do you want to support this candidate?"

"I don't," answered father. "I'm a man of my word, Squire Broderick. I told you long ago I'd have nothing to do with politics, and no more I will. If I am to be of any use, I must do it in another way—I must work from another level. The county may return what it likes for all I shall trouble about it."

"Well, 'pon my soul," began the Squire, but at that moment mother's voice came from the tea-table. She saw that a hot argument was imminent, and she never could abide an argument. I think that father too must have been disinclined for one, for when she said, "Father, your tea is poured out," he took the hint at once. The Squire looked disappointed for a moment, but I think he was so glad that father's influence was not going to take political shape against his candidate that he forgave all else.

Mother was just making Captain Forrester welcome beside her as the newest guest, when Deborah opened the door and ushered in Mr Hoad. I had quite forgotten that father had invited him. He stood a moment as it were appraising the company. His eye rested for less than an instant on Squire Broderick, on Captain Forrester, and then shifted immediately to mother.

"Oh, I am afraid that I intrude, Mrs Maliphant," said he.

"Not at all, not at all, Hoad," declared father. "Come in; we expected you."

Mother rose and offered him her hand. Then Captain Forrester, who had been looking at him, came forward and offered his too in his most genial manner. It was not till long afterwards that I found out that he made a special point of always being most genial to those people whom he considered ever so little beneath him.

"Oh, how are you, Hoad," said he. "I thought I recognised you, but I wasn't quite sure. I didn't expect to meet you here."

"No; nor I you!" exclaimed Hoad, gliding with ready adaptability into the position offered him—a quality which I think was perhaps his chief characteristic. "Delighted to see you."

Forrester gave up his place next mother, and sat down beside Joyce. The Squire just nodded to Mr Hoad, and then the conversation became general till the Squire and his nephew left, very shortly afterwards.

CHAPTER IX.

THREE weeks had passed since the day when Captain Forrester drove us out from town. Winter was gliding slowly into spring. The winds were still cold and piercing, and the bright sun and keen air sadly treacherous to sensitive folk, but the snow had all melted and the grass sprung green upon the marsh, throwing the blue of the sea beyond into sharp contrast; the cattle came out once more to feed; yellow-hammers and butcher-birds began to appear on the meadows; and over earth and sea, soft grey clouds broke into strange shapes upon the blue.

I remember all this now; then I was only conscious of one thing—that, in spite of the east wind, I was happy.

Father was well again: he rode over the

farm on his cob just as he used to do, and mother had forgotten the very name of a poultice. Joyce and the Captain showed every sign of playing in the romance that I had planned for them; no one had mentioned the subject of a bailiff for Knellestone from that day to this; and the Squire's ball was close at hand.

How was it possible that I should be otherwise than happy?

It was the very night before the dance. Jessie Hoad, who had consented to sing for our village concert, had been over, and we had been having a practice under Captain Forrester's directions. She was a fashionably-dressed, fashionably-mannered, fashionably-minded young woman, and quite content with herself; she generally resented directions, but she had submitted with a pretty good grace to his.

Miss Thorne had also been in. Joyce in this had shown one of those strange instances of obstinacy that were in her. Mary Thorne had asked to come, and she should not be refused. I remember noticing that Captain Forrester and that particularly gay-tempered young lady seemed to be very intimate together,—just, in fact, as people who had known one another from childhood would be. They took the liberty of telling one another home-truths,—at least Mary Thorne did (I fancied Frank responded less promptly), and did it in a blunt fashion that was peculiar to her. But I liked blunt people. I liked Mary Thorne very much.

Although she was an heiress to money that had been "sucked from the blood of the people"—to money made from a factory where girls and little children worked long hours out of the sunlight and the fresh air, —although she lived in a great house that overlooked acres of land that belonged to her,—and although my father could scarcely be got to speak to hers,—I liked Mary Thorne. She was so frank and jolly, and took it so as a matter of course that we were to be friends, that I always forgot that she rode in a carriage when I walked, and that she and I ought by rights not to be so much at ease.

That day she was particularly jolly, and she and I and Captain Forrester laughed together till I was quite ashamed to see that I had left Joyce all the entertaining of Miss Hoad to do in the meantime. For the Captain had not paid so much attention to Joyce on that day as on most others; I suppose he thought it was more discreet not to do so before strangers.

Both our lady visitors had left, however, by half-past five o'clock, and Captain Forrester stood on the garden-terrace now with Joyce alone, while I had returned to the darning of the family socks. It was close upon sunset, and they were looking at the lilacs that were beginning to swell in the bud. Joyce wore a lilac gown herself, I remember. The Captain had once admired it, and I had noticed that she had put it on very often since then.

I watched them from the parlour window where I sat with my work. For the first time I was half frightened at what I had done. I wondered what this romance was like that I had woven for Joyce. I felt that she was gliding away out of my ken, into an unknown world where I had driven her, and where I could not now follow her. Was it all happiness in that world?

Although the light was fading, and I wanted it all for my work, I moved away from the window-seat farther into the room. It seemed indelicate to watch them—although, indeed, they were only standing there side by side quietly, and what they were saying to one another I could not have heard if I had wished to do so. But it was my doing that they were alone at all. Joyce had stockings to darn too, but I had suggested that the parlour posy wanted freshening, and that there were some primroses out on the cliff.

Mother was out: she had gone to assist at the arrival of a new member of the population, and such an event always interested her so profoundly, that she forgot other things for the moment. Such an opportunity might not occur again for a long time, and I was not going to miss it,—otherwise those two had not been alone together before. At least, not to my knowledge.

Once Joyce had gone out into the village marketing by herself, and when she had come home she had run straight up into her room instead of coming into the parlour. I had gone up to her after a little while, as she did not come down, and had found her sitting by the window with her things still on, looking out to the sea with a half troubled expression on her face. I had asked her what was the matter, and she had smiled and said, " Nothing at all," and I had believed her.

However, even in the most open way in the world, Captain Forrester had managed to get pretty well acquainted with Joyce by this time, for he had come to the Grange almost every day since the Squire had brought him to pay that first call. He came on the plea of interest in father's views; and though mother, I could see, had taken a dislike to him, simply because he was a rival to the Squire, and took every opportunity of saying disparaging things about him to us girls when he was not present, even she felt the influence of the friendly manner that insisted on everything being pleasant and friendly in return, and did not seem somehow to be able to deny him the freedom which he claimed so naturally, of coming to the house whenever the fancy seized him. Certainly it would have been very difficult to turn Captain Forrester out.

Although it was evident enough to every one but father, in his dreamy self-absorption, that the young man came to see my beautiful sister, and was quickly falling hopelessly in love with her, still he was far too courteous to neglect others for her: he was always doing something for mother, procuring her something that she wanted, or in some way helping her; and as for me, he not only took all the burden of the village concert off my shoulders, the musical part of which always fell to my lot, but he also taught me how to sing my songs as I had no idea of how to sing them before, and took so much interest in my voice and in my performance that he really made me quite ambitious for the time as to what I might possibly do. And however much mother might have wished to turn the Captain out, there were difficulties attending this course of action.

In the first place, he was the Squire's nephew, and she could not very well be rude to the Squire's nephew, however much she may have fancied that the Squire would, in his heart, condone it; and then father had taken such an unusually strong fancy to the young man, that it would have been more than mother had ever been known to do to gainsay it. This friendship between an old and a young man was really a remarkable thing.

Father was not at all given to marked preferences for people: he was a reserved man, and his own society was generally sufficient for him. Even in the class whose interests he had so dearly at heart—his own class he would have called it, although in force and culture he was very far above the typical representatives of it—he was a god to the many rather than a friend to the individual. And apart from his friendship with the Squire, which was a friendship rather of custom than of choice, I do not remember his having a single intimate acquaintance. For I do not choose to consider that Hoad ever really was a friend in any sense of the word.

I have always fancied that father's capacity for friendship was swallowed up in that one romantic episode of his youth, that stood side by side with his love for our mother, and was not less beautiful though so different.

At first I think Forrester's aristocratic appearance, his knowledge of hunting and horseflesh, and music and dancing, and all the pleasures of the rich and idle, his polished manners, and even his good coat, rather stood in his light in the eyes of the "working man"; but it was only at first. Forrester's genuine enthusiasm for the interests that he affected, and his admiring deference for the mind that had thought the problem out, were enough to win the friendship of any man; for I suppose even at father's age one is not impervious to this refined sort of flattery.

Those were happy days in the dear old home, when we were all together, and none but the most trivial cloud had come to mar the harmony of our life.

I never remember father merrier than he was at that time. He and Frank would sit there smoking their pipes, and laughing and talking as it does one's heart good to remember. There was never any quarrelling over these discussions, as there used to be over the arguments with the Squire. Not that the young man always agreed at once about things. He required to be convinced, but then he always was convinced in the end. And his wild schemes for the development of the people, and the prevention of crime, and the alleviation of distress, all sounded so practical and pleasant, as set forth in his pleasant, brilliant language, full of fire and enthusiasm, and not at all like the same theories that father had been wont to quarrel over with the Squire in his sullen, serious fashion.

Everything that the Captain proposed was to be won from the top,—by discussions and meetings among the great of the land. He could shake hands on terms of equality with the poorest labourer over his pot of beer, but it was not from the labourer that the reform would ever be obtained; and he quite refused to see the matter in the sombre light in which father held it, who believed in no reform—if reform there could be—that did not come from the class that needed it, and that should come without bitter struggles and patient, dogged perseverance. And in the end he convinced—or seemed to convince—Frank that this was so.

I noticed how, imperceptibly, under the influence of father's earnest, powerful nature, the young man slowly became more earnest and more serious too. He talked less and he listened more; and truly there was no lack of food.

The great subjects under discussion were the nationalisation of land and the formation of trade corporations for the protection of the artisan class. These corporations were to be formed as far as possible on the model of the old guilds of the middle ages; they were to have compulsory provident funds for widows, orphans, and disabled workmen; they were to prevent labour on Sundays, and the employment of children and married women in factories; they were to determine the hours of labour and the rate of wages, and to inquire into the sanitary condition of work-places.

There were many other principles belonging to them besides these that I have quoted, but I cannot remember any more, though I remember clearly how father and Frank disagreed upon the question of whether the corporations were to enjoy a monopoly or not. I suppose they agreed finally upon the point, for I know that Frank undertook to air the matter at public meetings in London, and seemed to be quite sure that he would be able to start a trial society before long. I recollect how absolutely he refused to be damped by father's less sanguine mood; and best of all, I remember the smile that he brought to father's face, and the light that he called back to his drooping eye.

There was only one blot: the Squire did not come to see us. No doubt I should not have allowed at this time that it was any blot, and when mother remarked upon it, I held my tongue; but I know very well that I was sorry the Squire kept away.

On this evening of which I am thinking, however, the Squire did not keep away. I am afraid I had hurried a little over the darning of father's socks, that I might get to the making up of my own lace ruffles for the great event of the next night, and as I was sitting there in the window, making the most of the fading daylight, he came in. I heard him ask Deborah for father in the hall, and when she answered that she thought he was still out, he said he would wait and walked on into the parlour. He was free to come and go in our house. I fancied that he started a little when he saw me there alone; I suppose he expected to find the whole party as usual.

"Oh, how are you?" said he abruptly, holding out his hand without looking at me. "Is your mother out?"

I explained that mother had gone to the village to see a neighbour.

"I'll just wait a few minutes for your father," said he. "I want particularly to see him to-night."

"Is it about that young man?" asked I.

I do not know what possessed me to ask it. It was not becoming behaviour on my part, but at his words the recollection of that Mr Trayton Harrod, whom he had recommended to father as a bailiff, had suddenly returned to me. No mention having been made of him again, I had really scarcely remembered the matter till now, the excitement of the past three weeks had been so great.

He knit his brows in annoyance, and I was sorry I had spoken.

"What young man?" asked he.

"That gentleman whom you recommended to father for the farm," said I, half ashamed of myself.

"Oh, Trayton Harrod!" exclaimed the Squire, with a relieved expression. "Oh no, no, I shall not trouble your father again about that unless he speaks to me. I thought it might be an advantageous thing, for I have known the young man since he was a lad, and he has been well brought up,—a clever fellow all round. But your father knows his own business best. It might not work."

It was on my lips to say that of course it would not work, but I restrained myself, and the Squire went on.

"I'm so delighted to see your father himself again," he said. "There's no need for any one to help him so long as he can do it all himself; and of course you, I know, do a great deal for him," added he, as though struck by an after-thought. "I saw you walking round the mill farm this morning."

"Did you?" answered I. "I only went up about the flour. I didn't see you."

"No," he said. "I was riding the other way."

He walked up to the window as he spoke, and looked out over the lawn.

Somehow I was glad that I had just seen Joyce and Captain Forrester go down the cliff out of sight a few minutes before the Squire arrived.

"Everybody out?" asked he.

"Yes," answered I. "Everybody."

He did not ask whether his nephew had been there. He drew a chair up to the table and began playing with the reels and tapes in my work-basket. Mother and Joyce would have been in an agony at seeing their sacred precincts invaded by the cruel hand of man, but it rather amused me to see the hopeless mess into which he was getting the hooks and silks and needles.

My basket never was a miracle of orderliness at any time.

"Is Miss Joyce quite well," said he at last, trying to get the scissors free of a train of cotton in which he had entangled them.

I felt almost inclined to laugh. Even to me, who am awkward enough, this seemed such an awkward way of introducing the subject, for of course I had guessed that he had missed her directly he had come into the room.

"Yes, quite well, thank you," answered I. And then I added, laughing, and seeing that he had got hold of a bit of my lace, "Oh, take care, please; that's a bit of my finery for to-morrow night."

He dropped it as if it had burned him. "Oh dear, dear, yes,—how clumsy I am!" cried he, pushing the work-basket far from him. "I hope I have spoilt nothing."

"Why, no, of course not," laughed I. "I oughtn't to have spoken. But you see I have only got that one bit of lace, and I want it for to-morrow night."

"Oh yes; I suppose you young ladies are going to be very grand indeed," smiled he.

"Oh no, not grand," insisted I; "but very jolly. We mean to enjoy ourselves, I can tell you."

"That's right," said he. "So do I."

But he could not get away from the subject of Joyce.

"Has your sister gone far?" asked he in a minute.

"I don't know," I answered, quite determined to throw no light upon the subject of where she was and with whom.

A direct question made it difficult now to keep to this determination.

"Do you know if my nephew has been here this afternoon?" was the question.

I looked down intently at my work.

"Yes, he came," answered I. "He sat some while with father, till father went out."

I did not add any mention of where he had been since. It was a prevarication of course, but I thought I did it out of a desire to spare the Squire's feelings. He asked no more questions. He sat silent for a while.

"Your father and Frank seem to be great friends," observed he presently, and I fancied a little bitterly.

"Yes," I replied; "Captain Forrester has quite picked father's spirits up. He has been a different man since he had him to sympathise with over his pet schemes."

I felt directly I had said the words that they were inconsiderate words, and I regretted them, but I could not take them back.

Squire Broderick flushed over his fair white brow.

"Yes; my nephew professes to be as keen after all these democratic dodges as your father himself," he said curtly.

"Oh, it's not that," cried I, anxious to mend matters. "Father doesn't need to have everybody agree with him for him to be friends with them."

"No, I quite understand," answered the Squire, beginning again on the unlucky basket. And after a pause he added, as though with an effort, "Frank is a very delightful companion, I know; and when he brings his enthusiasm to bear upon subjects that are after one's own heart, it is naturally very pleasant."

"Yes," I agreed. "That's just it, he is

so very enthusiastic. He would make such a splendid speaker, such a splendid leader of some great democratic movement."

The Squire left my work-basket in the muddle in which he had finally put it, and stuck his hands into his pockets.

"Do you think so?" he said.

"Oh yes, I'm sure of it," continued I, blindly. "And I am sure father thinks so too."

"Indeed!" answered the Squire, I thought a little scornfully. "And, pray, how is my nephew going to be a great democratic leader? Is he going into Parliament? Is he going to contest the county at the next election?"

"Why, how can you think he would do such a thing, Mr Broderick," exclaimed I, "when he knows that you are supporting the opposite side?"

"Oh, that would be no objection," said the Squire, still in the same tone of voice. "The objection would be that a Radical stands such a small chance of getting in."

"Besides," added I, collecting myself, "I am sure he has no wish to go into Parliament.

Father and he both agree that a man can do a great deal more good out of Parliament than in it. They say that the finest leaders that there have been in all nations have been those who have got at the people straight — without any humbug between them."

"Pooh!" said the Squire. Then controlling himself, he added, "Well, and does Frank think that he is going to get at the people that way? Does he suppose it will cost him nothing?"

"Oh no; I suppose it will cost money," assented I.

"Ah!" said the Squire, in the tone of a man who has got to the bottom of the question at last. "Well, then, I think it's only fair that your father should know that there is very little chance of Frank's being of any use to him. If he is pinning his faith on Frank as a possible representative of his convictions, he is making a mistake, and it is only right that he should be warned. Frank has no money of his own—no money at all. He has nothing but his captain's pay, and that isn't enough for him to keep himself upon."

The Squire spoke bitterly. Even I, girl as I was, could see that something had annoyed him to the point of making him lose control over himself.

"I don't think father has pinned his faith on Captain Forrester," said I, half vexed. "I don't think there has been any question between them such as you fancy. I think they are merely fond of discussing matters upon which they agree. At all events, I am sure it has never entered father's head to consider whether Captain Forrester had money or not."

"Well, I think, for several reasons, it is just as well there should be no mistake about the thing," repeated the Squire vehemently, walking up and down the room in his excitement. "Frank has no money and no prospects, excepting those which he may make for himself. I sincerely hope that he may do something better than marry an heiress, which is his mother's aim for him, but meanwhile he certainly has very little property excepting his debts."

A light suddenly broke upon me. The words, "marry an heiress," had suddenly flashed a meaning on Squire Broderick's strange attitude. He was afraid that Captain Forrester was winning Joyce's affections. He was jealous. I would not have believed it of him; but perhaps, of course, it was natural. I was sorry for him. The remembrance of the sad bereavements of his youth made me sorry for him.

After all, though I did not then consider him a young man, it was sad to have done with life so early,—to have no chance of another little heir to the acres that he owned, instead of that poor little baby of whom mother had told us. For, of course, there was no chance of that, and Captain Forrester would finally inherit them. I had not thought of that before. No wonder he was bitter, and I was sorry for him. He spoke no more after that last speech. He came and stood over me where I was working.

"But, after all," said he presently, in his natural genial tones, "I don't know why I troubled you with all that. You are scarcely the person whom it should interest. I beg your pardon."

I did not know what to say, so I said nothing.

The Squire moved to the window, and I put down my work and followed him. The daylight had gone; there was no more sewing to be done that evening without a lamp. As I came forward I saw the tall, slight figure of Captain Forrester standing up against the dim blue of the twilight sky, and holding out his hand to help my sister up the last, steepest bit of the ascent to our lawn. I glanced at the Squire. His face was not sad nor sorry, but it was angry. He turned away from the window, and so did I, and as we faced round we saw mother standing in the doorway. She had her bonnet and cloak still on; she must have come in quietly by the back-door, as she had a habit of doing, while we were talking. How much had she heard of what the Squire had said?

He went up to her and bade her good-day and good-bye in one breath. He said he would not wait longer to see father. He went out and away without meeting his nephew. I was very glad that he did, for thus mother went up-stairs at once to take off her things, and being in a garrulous frame of mind, from her experiences of the afternoon with the new-born baby, she stayed up-stairs some time talking to Deborah, and did not come down to the parlour again till after Captain Forrester had taken his leave. So she never knew anything of that long half-hour spent upon the garden cliff at the sun-setting.

CHAPTER X.

I THINK I saw the dawn that day on which the ball was to be. Whether I did or not, the morning was still very grey and cold when I crept out of my bed and stole to the wardrobe to look at our two dresses. There they hung, carefully displayed upon shifting pegs such as were used in old-fashioned presses : one soft white muslin, the other of that pale apple-green shot silk which had belonged to mother in the days of her youth, and which I had been allowed to make up for the occasion. We had worked at them for days.

Joyce was clever at dressmaking : she was clever at all things that needed deftness of fingers. She had fitted me with my frock, and we had both worked together. But now the dresses were finished, the last ruffle had been tacked in; there was nothing more to do, and the day wore away very slowly till evening.

At last the hour came when it was time to dress, and such a washing of faces and brushing of hair as went on in that little attic chamber for half an hour, no one would believe.

Joyce insisted on "finishing" me first. She coiled up my hair at the back of my head, brushing it as neatly as she could, and laying it in two thick bands on either side of my temples. It never will look very neat, it is such vigorous unruly hair, this red hair of mine, and to this day always has tendrils escaping here and there over forehead and neck. But she did her best for it, and I was pleased with myself. I was still more pleased with myself when I got on the green shot silk with the lace ruffles. Joyce said she was surprised to see what a change it made in me. So was I.

My skin was very pink and white wherever it was not spoilt by freckles, and the green of the frock seemed to show it up and make the red lips look redder than ever. It is true that my neck and arms were frail still with the frailness of youth, but then my figure was slim too, and my eyes were black with excitement, and shone till they were twice their usual size. I thought, as I looked in the glass, that I was not so very plain. Yes, I was right when I had begged the shot silk. Joyce could wear anything, but I, who was no "fine bird" by nature, needed the "fine feathers."

I was pleased with myself, and I smiled with satisfaction when Joyce declared again that she was quite surprised to see what a good appearance I had. "If you would only keep yourself tidy, Margaret, you have no idea how much better you would look," said she.

It was what Deborah was always saying, but I did not resent it from Joyce. She was gentle in her way of saying it; and I remember that I promised I would brush my hair smooth in future, and wear my collars more daintily. I do not believe that I kept to my resolution, but that evening I was not at all the Margaret of everyday life as I surveyed myself in the glass.

"But come," said I, hurriedly — half ashamed of myself, I do believe—"we shall be late if we don't make haste. Do get on, Joyce."

Joyce began brushing out her long golden hair—real gold hair, not faint flaxen—and coiled the smooth shining bands of it round her little head. It was a little head, such as I have seen in the pictures of the Virgins painted by Italian painters of long ago.

"I shan't be long," said she.

I sat down and watched her. She would not have let me help her if I had wanted to do so. She would have said that I should only disarrange myself, and that I should be of no use. Certainly nothing was wanted but what she did for herself, and she did it quickly enough. When she stood up before the mirror—tipped back to show the most of her person, for we had no pier-glasses at the Grange—I do not believe that any one could have found a thing to improve in her. Her figure looked taller and slenderer than ever in the long white dress, and the soft little folds of the muslin clung tenderly around her delicate shape, just leaving bare her neck and arms, that were firm and white as alabaster. Her face was flushed as a May rose; her lips were parted in her anxiety to hasten, and showed the little even white teeth within. Her blue eyes were clear and soft under the black lashes.

She moved before the glass to see that her dress was not too long, and bent back her slender throat, upon which she had just clasped mother's delicate little old-fashioned gold necklace with the drops of yellow beryl-stone. It was the only bit of good jewellery in the family, and Joyce always wore it, it became her so well.

"Come now, Meg," said she, "I am quite ready. Let's go and see if we can do anything to help mother."

We went down-stairs. Deborah was there in mother's room waiting to survey us all. She had just fastened mother's dove-coloured satin gown that had served her for every party she had been at since she was married. Mother had just the same shaped cap on that she always wore; she never would alter it for any fashion, but that night the frill of it was made of beautiful old lace that she kept in blue paper and lavender all the rest of the year. I thought she looked splendid, but Joyce was not so easily pleased.

"Dear mother, you really must have another gown before you go anywhere again," said she, shaking out the skirt with a dissatisfied air. "This satin has lost all its stiffness."

Mother looked at it a little anxiously herself, I remember, when Joyce said this. We considered Joyce a judge of dress and the fashions, and of course the Squire's ball was a great occasion. But she said she thought it did very well for an old lady, and indeed so did I, although that may perhaps have been because I was very anxious to be off.

Dear mother! I do not think she gave much thought to herself; she was taken up with pride in us. Yes, I do believe that night she was proud even of me.

She smiled when Deborah, with her hand on the door knob, said patronisingly that although she did not hold with bare arms and necks for modest females, she never would have thought that I should have "dressed up" so well. Mother bade her begone, but I think she was pleased.

"Dear me!" said she, looking at me. "I recollect buying that silk. It must have been in '52, when father took me up to town to see the Exhibition. It was cheap for the good silk it is. It has made up very well."

She turned me all round. Then she went to her jewel-case, unlocked it, and took out a row of red coral beads.

"That's what you want with that dress," said she, fastening them round my throat. "And you shall have them for your own. Red-haired women ought to wear coral, folk say. Though, for my part, I always thought it was putting on too many colours."

How well I remember my pleasure at that gift! Joyce wanted to persuade me not to wear them; she said the pale green of the frock was prettier without the red beads. But I wouldn't listen to her; I was too pleased with them, and I do not believe that it was entirely owing to gratified vanity: I think a little of it was pleasure that mother thought my appearance worth caring for.

I should not have thought it worth caring

for myself two days ago, and I should not have cared whether mother did or not. But something had happened to me. Was it the sight of Joyce and her lover that had made me think of myself as a woman? I cannot tell. All I know is, that when we walked into the Squire's ball-room a quarter of an hour afterwards, I felt my face flame as I saw his gaze rest upon me for a moment, and I longed most heartily to be back again in my high-necked homespun frock, with no corals round my throat at all. So inconsistent are we at nineteen!

Fortunately my awakening self-consciousness was soon put to flight by other more engrossing emotions. There was a fair sprinkling of people already when we got into the room, and more were arriving every moment. Mr Farnham and the maiden sister with whom he lived were going busily about welcoming the Squire's guests almost as though they were the host and hostess themselves: he was the Conservative member. A quiet, inoffensive old gentleman himself, who would have been nothing and nobody without the Squire; but blessed with a most officious lady for relative, who took the whole neighbourhood under her wing.

She rather annoyed me by the way she had of trading on the Squire's support of her brother. He supported her brother because he was a Conservative, not at all because he was Mr Farnham, or even Miss Farnham's brother.

Poor Mr Broderick! I daresay, if the truth had been known, he must often heartily have longed to get rid of them. But the old thing was a good soul in her way, if it *was* a dictatorial, loud-voiced way, and was very active among the poor, although it was not always in the manner which they liked.

She and mother invariably quarrelled over the advantages of soup-kitchens and clothing clubs; for mother was every bit as obstinate as Miss Farnham, and being an old-fashioned woman, liked to do her charity in a more personal fashion.

I looked with mingled awe and amusement upon their meeting to-night. Miss Farnham had an aggressive sort of headdress, with nodding artificial flowers that seemed to look down scornfully upon mother's old lace and soft frills. She had not seen me for some time, and when mother introduced me as her youngest daughter, she took my hand firmly in hers, and held it awhile in her uncompromising grip while she looked at me through and through.

"Well, I never saw such a thing in my life!" exclaimed she presently, in a loud voice that attracted every one's attention.

I blushed. I was not given to blushing, but it was enough to make any one blush. I thought, of course, that she was alluding to my attire, in which I had felt so shy and awkward from the moment that I had entered the ball-room, from the moment that I had felt the Squire's glance rest upon my neck and arms.

She dropped my hand.

"The very image of him," said she, turning to mother.

"Yes, she is very like her father," agreed the mother.

"Why, my dear, the very image of him," repeated the aggravating creature. "Got his temper too?" asked she, turning to me again.

"I don't know, ma'am, I'm sure," answered I, half amused, but still more annoyed. "I daresay."

"Oh, I'll be bound you have, and proud of it too," declared she, shaking her head emphatically. "Girls are always proud to be like their fathers."

"I don't suppose it'll make any very particular difference who I'm like," said I. "Things will happen just the same, I expect."

Miss Farnham laughed, and patted me boisterously on the back.

I do not think she was an ill-natured woman, although she certainly had the talent of making one feel very uncomfortable.

"Well, you're not so handsome as your sister," added she. "But I don't know that you hadn't better thank your stars for that."

With that she turned away from me and sat down beside mother, arranging her dress comfortably over her knees as though she meant to stay there the whole evening.

The people kept coming fast now. The Squire stood at the door shaking hands as hard as he could. There was the old village doctor with his pretty grand-daughter, and the young village doctor who had inherited the practice, and had just married a spry little wife in the hope of making it more important.

And then there was the widow of an officer, who lived in a solid brick house that stood at the corner of the village street, and had two sons in the ship business in town. And there was the mild-eyed clergyman with his delicate young wife, who had more than enough babies of her own, and was only too thankful to leave the babies of the parish to Miss Farnham or any one else who would mother them.

She was a sweet little woman, with a transparently white face and soft silky hair, and she wore her wedding-dress to-night, without the slightest regard to the fact that it was made in a somewhat elaborate fashion of six years back, and was not exactly suited to her figure at that particular moment. She sat down between mother and Miss Farnham, and must have been considerably cheered by that lady's remark to the effect that she looked as if she ought to be in her bed, and that if she did not retire to it she would most likely soon be in her grave.

I left mother and went up to greet Mary Thorne, who had just come in with her father. He was a great, strong, florid man, rather shaky about his *h*'s, but very much the reverse of shaky in any other way; shrewd and keen as a sharp knife or an east wind.

I don't know that I ever spoke to him but this once in my life. Father had such an overpowering aversion to him that we were not allowed to keep even the daughter's acquaintance long after this, but he made the impression on me that there was only one soft spot in him, and that for the motherless girl who was the only person allowed to contradict him.

She contradicted him now.

The Squire had gone up to receive them, bluntly enough even I could see; but the Squire might be allowed to have an aversion to the man who was going in as a Radical to contest his Conservative's long-occupied seat, though indeed I believe his dislike to the manufacturer was quite as much because he had bought up one of the old places in the neighbourhood with money earned in business. I fancy the Thornes were only invited that night as old friends of Frank Forrester's, and I don't think Frank was thanked for the necessity.

"You must have had a rare job, Broderick, lighting this old place up," he was saying as I came up. "All this dark oak, so gloomy looking."

"Oh, papa, how can you!" laughed his daughter. "Why, it's what everybody admires. It's the great sight of the whole neighbourhood."

"Yes, yes, I know my dear," answered Mr Thorne. "You mean to say that we should like to live here ourselves. Well, yes, I should have bought the place if it had been in the market, but——"

"But you would have done it up," broke in the Squire, bristling all over, "whereas there's been nothing new in the Manor since——"

He stopped.

I fancied that he was going to say, "since I brought my bride home," but he said, after a pause, "since my father died."

"Well, to be sure I do like a bit of brightness and colour," acknowledged Thorne, whose fine house, although in excellent taste, was decidedly ornate and splendid; "and it is more suited to festal occasions."

"There, papa, you know nothing about it," declared Mary emphatically. "I declare, I never saw the Manor look better. Those flags and garlands are beautiful."

"Oh, my nephew Frank did all that," answered the Squire carelessly. "He likes that sort of thing."

"Captain Forrester," repeated the girl, with just a little smile on her frank, fresh face. "Well, it does him credit, then. It isn't every one would take so much trouble."

"He likes taking trouble," said I. "Just look at the trouble that he has taken over our concert."

"He likes playing first fiddle," laughed Miss Thorne gaily, her rosy face—that was too rosy for prettiness, although not too rosy for the perfection of health—flushing rosier than ever as she said it. "I always tell him so."

I did not answer. Mr Thorne and his daughter moved on, and I looked round the room in search of the Captain. The place did look very beautiful, although I do not think that I should like now to see its severe proportions and splendid wood wainscoting disfigured by flags and garlands. We were dancing in what used long ago to be the monks' refectory. The house had been built on the site of a part of the monastic buildings belonging to the Abbey, and this portion of the old edifice had been retained, while the remainder of the house was in Tudor style. I heard the Squire explaining it to the new parson, who had lately come to the next parish. I had heard him explain it before, or I do not suppose that I should have known anything at all about it.

"I suppose you consider it shocking to be dancing in any part of the monastery," I could hear him say, laughing; "but it isn't so bad as a friend of mine, who gives balls in what used to be the chapel."

The parson was a young man with a sallow shaven face and very refined features: the expression of his mouth was gentle, almost tremulous, but his eyes were dark and penetrating.

"I'm not quite so prejudiced as that," he said, laughing also, "although I do wear the cloth."

"That's right," said the Squire heartily. "We have the remains of a thirteenth-century chapel of the purest period in the grounds, and we don't desecrate that even by a school-feast. You must come and see it in the day-time."

Father came up at that moment. He felt dreadfully like a fish out of water, poor father, in this assembly, and looked it. The Squire in a hasty fashion introduced him to the Rev. Cyril Morgan, and passed on to shake hands with a portly wine merchant, who had lately retired from business in the neighbouring town, and had taken one of the solid red-brick houses that were the remnants of our town's affluence.

This gentleman introduced his wife, and she had to be introduced to the company, and the host's hands were full. Father moved away with the parson. He seemed rather disgusted at first, but the young man looked at him with a smile upon his gentle mouth and in his dark eyes, and said diffidently, "I have heard a great deal of you, Mr Maliphant,—the whole neighbourhood rings with your name. I am proud to meet you."

Of course I liked that young man at once, and as I went to sit down again beside the mother and Joyce, I was pleased to see across the room that father and the Rev. Cyril Morgan had entered upon a conversation. But, to tell the truth, I soon forgot him,—I was too busy looking about me.

I could not help wondering where Captain Forrester could be, and I was quite angry with Joyce for being so dignified and seeming to care so little. She seemed to be quite engrossed with the Hoad girls, who sailed in followed by their father, just late enough to be fashionable, and to secure a good effect for their smart new frocks.

I am afraid I was not gracious to the Hoads. I could not be so gracious as Joyce, who took all their patronising over the concert in the utmost good faith. I turned away from them, and continued my search for Joyce's admirer. I disliked them, and I am afraid that I showed it.

But they passed on,—Bella, who was the

better looking of the two, pursued by two town-bred youths asking for a place on her card; Jessie, the elder, talking with an old lady of title from the seaport town, who wished her to sing at a charity concert.

They seemed to be very much engrossed; nevertheless, when presently the band struck up the first waltz, they, as well as many other people in the room, turned round to look who was dancing it. They put up their long-handled eye-glasses and fairly stared. For as soon as the music began the Squire had walked up to my sister and had asked her to open the ball with him.

Mother blushed with pleasure and triumph; her dear blue eyes positively shone. She did not say a word, but I know that if she had spoken she would have said that she was not surprised.

I was not surprised either, but I was very much annoyed, and I was not at all in a good temper with Captain Forrester when, two minutes afterwards, he appeared coming out of the conservatory with Mary Thorne upon his arm. What had he been about? No wonder that his face clouded when he saw that he was too late. But it was his own fault. I was not a bit sorry for him. Mary Thorne was laughing, and looking up half-defiantly in his face. She looked as if she were saying one of those rough blunt things of which she was so fond; and she might well say one at this moment to Captain Forrester, although I scarcely supposed it could be on the topic on which he deserved it.

Could she possibly be chaffing him on having missed the first dance with my sister? No; for she had had no opportunity of noticing his devotion to her. She dropped his arm and nodded to him merrily, as much as to bid him leave her,—as much as to say that she knew there might be better sport elsewhere. And after a word in reply to what she had said, he did leave her and came across to me.

There was a troubled, preoccupied look on his bright face which was scarcely accounted for by the fact that he had missed a dance with Joyce. He greeted me and sat down beside me without even asking after father. We sat and watched Joyce float round in the strong grasp of the Squire, but I do not think that we were either of us quite so pleased at the sight as was mother, upon whose face was joy unalloyed.

She was simply genuinely proud that the Squire should have opened the ball with her daughter. I think she would have been proud of it had there been no deeper hopes at the bottom of her heart. But there were deeper hopes, and as I watched Joyce that night I remembered them.

In the excitement of watching the romance that I had fancied developing itself more quickly and more decisively than I had even hoped, I had at first quite forgotten my fears about the Squire wanting to marry Joyce. They had not occurred to my mind at all until that afternoon two days ago when he had talked so vehemently about Frank's position. But now, as I watched him with her, the notion which I had rather refused to entertain at all before took firmer shape.

I was afraid that the Squire really did mean something by this very marked attention to his tenant's daughter. It must needs excite a great deal of comment even amongst those who knew our rather particular position in the village, and the unusual intimacy between two families of different social standing. Would he have courted that comment merely for the sake of gratifying his old friend? What if he should propose to Joyce—if he should ask our parents' consent to the marriage at once? Would Captain Forrester, the unknown stranger, have any chance beside the friend of years? Would the soldier, who had nothing but what he earned by his brave calling, have a chance against the man who could give her as fine a home as any in the county?

Not with mother; no, I felt not for an instant with mother. But with father——?

I knew very well that father, whatever his respect for the man, would never see a marriage between the Squire and his daughter with pleasure,—and I even thought it likely that he would downright forbid it. But what would be his feelings with regard to the Captain? Would they be any different because, belonging by birth to another class, he yet desired to work for the interest of the class that was ours? I could not tell.

I was roused from my dream by the voice

of Captain Forrester at my side. He was asking me for a dance—this very next one. There was something in the tone of his voice that puzzled me,—a harsh sound, as though something hurt him. Of course I gave him the dance. I was only too delighted.

My feet had begun to itch as soon as I had heard the music, and when I had seen Joyce sailing round, and no one had come to ask me, I had felt very lonely. We stood up, even before the Squire had brought Joyce back to mother,—we stood up, and with the first bars of the new waltz we set forth. I soon forgot all thought of Joyce or any one else in the pure joy of my own pleasure.

I did love dancing. I did not remember that it was Captain Forrester with whom I was dancing, I only knew that it was a man who held me firmly, and whose limbs moved with mine in an even and dreamy rhythm as we glided across something that scarcely seemed to be a floor, to the slow lilt of magic music. I was very fond of dancing. I suppose Captain Forrester guessed it, for he never paused once the whole dance through.

When we stopped, just pleasantly out of breath, as the last chords died slowly away, he said, with his eyes on my face in that way that I have described, " Why, Miss Maliphant, you are a heavenly dancer. Where did you learn it?"

"I had six lessons at the academy in the town," answered I gravely, and I wondered why he burst out laughing; "but Joyce gets out of breath sooner than I do, although she had twelve lessons."

The laughter faded out of his face as I mentioned Joyce's name.

"I don't mean to say that Joyce doesn't dance beautifully," I added hastily; "she dances better than I do, because she is so tall and slight, but she does get out of breath before the end of a waltz."

He did not make any remark upon this. He only said, "Shall we go back to your mother?"

We got up and walked across the room. Miss Thorne was talking to mother, and a clean-shaven, fresh-coloured young officer was inscribing his name on Joyce's programme.

Captain Forrester just shook hands with

Joyce, and then he came and sat down beside mother and began talking away to her in his most excited fashion, telling her all about the waxing of the floor and the hanging of the banners and the trimming of the evergreen garlands, and how the gardener would put the Union Jack upside down, until she was forced to be more gracious with him than was her wont.

Joyce's sweet mouth had the look upon it that I knew well when mother and she had had an uncomfortable passage, but I could not imagine why she should wear it to-night. I could look across upon her programme, and I could see that there were names written nearly all the way down it, although I could not read whose names they were, and, especially after my one taste of the joy of waltzing, I was beginning to think that no girl could have cause for sadness who had partners for every dance. Alas! I had but one, and my spirits were beginning to sink very low. I had forgotten love-affairs; I wanted to waltz.

"There is a dreadful lack of gentlemen," said Jessie Hoad, who had come up beside us, putting up her eyeglass and looking round the room. "That unfortunate man must have his hands full."

"Do you mean Squire Broderick?" asked Miss Thorne. "I don't think he considers himself unfortunate. He looked cheerful enough just now dancing with Miss Maliphant."

Miss Hoad vouchsafed no reply to this; she moved off to where her father was talking to mine in a corner, and passing her arm within his, walked him off without the slightest ceremony to be introduced to the old lady with the handle to her name who had come over from our fashionable seaport.

I thought it was very rude, but Mr Hoad was not quite as affable himself to-night as he was in the privacy of our own Grange parlour.

"I hate that kind of thing," said Miss Thorne to me in her outspoken way. "When are there ever men enough at a country dance unless you get in the riff-raff from behind the shop-counters? We come to meet our friends, not to whirl round with mere sticks."

I thought it was very nice of Miss Thorne, but I wished there were just men enough to dance with me.

The music struck up again, and Joyce went off with her partner. I felt as though life indeed were altogether a disappointment; and it did not give me any pleasure to hear Miss Thorne commenting upon Joyce's beauty, nor laughing in her frank, good-natured way about the Squire's attentions, any the more than it amused me to hear fragments of the gay descriptions with which Captain Forrester was making the time pass for mother.

But, after all, I began to despair too soon; it was only the fourth dance of the evening. Before it was over the Squire came up to me.

"I have been so busy," said he, "I haven't been able to come before, but I hope you haven't given all your dances away?"

Although I was new to the ways of the world, an instinct within taught me to say coolly, "Oh no, not all."

"What can you give me?" asked he. And he quoted three numbers further on in the evening. "I think, being old friends, we might dance three dances together," added he with a smile.

"Oh yes," cried I. "I should like to dance them with you."

The Squire was a beautiful dancer, although he was not a young man—or rather, although he was not what I then considered a young man. I fancied he did not smile at my enthusiastic reply. He even looked rather grave. I was too simple to think of not giving him my programme. I saw him glance at it and then at me. From that moment I did not lack partners, and, as far as the company could provide them, good ones.

To be sure I jostled round the room with a raw youth or two, and guided a puffing gentleman through the maze, and let my toes be trodden upon by a tall gentleman with glasses on his nose, who only turned round when he thought of it; but on the whole I enjoyed myself, and it was all thanks to my host. I scarcely knew a man when I went into the room, and certainly, save for that one wild delightful waltz, Captain Forrester had taken no account of me, although he had sat close to me half the evening, and one would have thought he would have noticed that I was not dancing. But then, of course, he was preoccupied. I could not make him out at all. All the evening I could not once catch him even talking to Joyce, and I am quite sure that when I went in to supper he had not asked her to dance once.

If I had been enjoying myself less I might have thought more of it, but I was too happy to remember it until the breathing-time came, when I went into the dining-room. Then, when I saw Captain Forrester sitting in one of the best places with that horrid old Miss Farnham, and Joyce at a side table, with scarcely room to stand, and no one but my pet aversion, Mr Hoad, even to get her something to eat, my blood boiled, and I could scarcely speak civilly to him.

And he seemed so interested too, so wrapt up in what the silly creature was saying, with that nodding old top-knot of hers! I was thankful when he rose and took her outside to finish their discussion about the poor-laws in the seclusion of some corner of the drawing-room. I was very angry with him.

I looked suspiciously at the Squire, who had taken mother in to supper and sat at the head of the table with her. Mother was smiling happily: she was proud of the honour that the Squire was doing to her and hers. But I could not look kindly at the Squire. It was infamous if, out of mere jealousy, he had tried to spoil two lives. Instead of being proud that he had done my sister the honour of opening the ball with her—instead of being grateful to him for his kindness to me, and pleased to see all the attention that he was paying to our mother amidst the county magnates whom he might have preferred,—I was eaten up with this new idea, and felt my heart swell within me as Joyce passed me presently, with that calm and yet half-tired look on her beautiful face.

Midnight was long past, and it was nearly time to go home. In fact, father had said that it was time to go home long ago. He had made a new friend in the young parson, and seemed to have passed an hour happily with him, but the parson had left, and he had exhausted every argument that he would consent to discuss with the people whom he met in ordinary society, and had been persuaded by Mr Hoad to speak a civil word on commonplace subjects to his pet aversion Mr Thorne, and now he was thoroughly sick of the whole thing, and would have no more to do with it.

He came up to mother and begged her to come home, but mother had heard the Squire ask Joyce for another dance later on, and I knew very well that she would not leave till that was through : besides, she was the most unselfish old dear in the world, for all her rough words sometimes, and would never have consented to deprive us of an inch of pleasure that she could procure us.

Personally I was very grateful to her. I had a dance left with the Squire myself, and besides the pleasure of it, I had been arranging something that I wanted to say to him. I was standing alone in the entrance to the conservatory when he came to claim it. I was looking for Joyce. I had missed her ever since supper. I had thought—I had hoped—that she was with Captain Forrester; but when Miss Thorne told me he was talking politics with Mr Hoad in the drawing-room, I believed her, and was at a loss to understand my sister's absence. Could she be unwell? But I did not confide my doubts to the Squire. He put his arm around me and swept me off on to that lovely floor, and I thought of nothing else.

I remember very clearly how well the Squire looked that night,—fresh and merry, with bright keen eyes.

"That's a pretty frock, Miss Margaret," said he, as we were waltzing round.

"Oh, I'm so glad you like it," answered I; "I was afraid it wasn't suitable."

In the excitement of the ball I had entirely forgotten all about my appearance, but now that the Squire remarked upon it, I remembered how uncomfortable I had felt in it at first.

"Why not suitable?" asked he.

"Mother bought it at the great Exhibition in '52," said I.

But the real cause of the awkwardness of my feeling had arisen from the fact that I felt unlike myself in a "party frock," and not at all from any fear that the frock might be old-fashioned.

"Oh! and Miss Hoad considers that an objection, I suppose," smiled he. "Well, I don't. There's only one thing I don't like," added he in his most downright manner—"I don't like the trinkets. You're too young for trinkets."

He had felt it. He had felt just what I had felt—that it was unsuitable for a girl like me to be dressed up.

"You mean the corals," said I; and my voice sank a little, for I was proud of the corals too, and pleased that mother should have given them to me.

"Yes," he answered. "They are very pretty; but," he added gently, "a young girl's neck is so much prettier."

We waltzed round two turns without speaking. Then he said abruptly, "Perhaps, by the way, I ought not to have said that, but I think such old friends as we are may say anything to one another, mayn't we?"

"Why, of course," said I, rather surprised.

The speech was not at all like one of the Squire's. I had always thought that he said just whatever he liked to any of us. But to be sure, until the other evening, he had never spoken very much to me at all.

I laughed—a little nervous laugh. I was stupidly nervous that night with the Squire. "I think we should be very silly if we didn't say whatever came into our heads," said I. "I don't think I like people who don't say what they think. Although, of course, it is much more difficult for me to say things to you, than for you to say them to me."

"Why?" asked he.

"Well, of course, because you're so much older," answered I.

He was silent. For a moment the high spirits that I had so specially noticed in him seemed to desert him.

"Well, what do you want to say to me that's disagreeable," said he presently, with a little laugh.

"Oh, nothing disagreeable," declared I. "It's about your nephew, Captain Forrester."

"Oh!" said he.

His expression changed. It was as though I had not said what he had expected me to say. But his brow clouded yet more, only it was more with anger than sadness,—the same look of anger that he had worn the other afternoon. He certainly was a very hot-tempered man.

"I don't think you are fair to him," said I boldly.

He looked at me. He smiled a little.

"In what way not fair to him?" said he.

"Well, if it had been any one else but me," answered I, "and you had said all that you did say the other day in the Grange parlour, I think the person would have been set against Captain Forrester. Of course it made no difference to me, because I like him so much."

He winced I fancied.

"You don't understand, my dear young lady," said he. "I merely wished that there should be no misunderstandings."

"I don't think there were any misunderstandings," answered I. "We always knew that Captain Forrester was not a man of property. He told us so himself."

"Well, then, that's all right," said the Squire.

"We liked him rather the better for it," concluded I, prompted by a wicked spirit of mischief.

The Squire did not reply to this. Of course there was nothing to reply to it. It was a rude speech, and was better taken no notice of. He merely put his arm round my waist again, and asked if we should finish the waltz. I was sorry for my discourtesy before we had done, and tried to make up for it.

Although the weather was still very treacherous in spite of the clear sky, couples had strayed out through the conservatory on to the broad terrace outside. I suggested to the Squire that we should do the same. He demurred at first, saying it was too cold; but as I laughed at this, and ran outside without any covering over me, he came after me —but he passed through the entrance-hall on his way and fetched a cloak, which he wrapped round me. In spite of my naughtiness, he had that care for the daughter of his old friends.

The moon was shining outside. It made dark shadows and white lights upon the ivied walls and upon the slender grey pillars of the ruined chapel : within, beneath the pointed arches, black patches lay upon the grass, alternated with sharp contrasts of lights where the moonbeams streamed in through the chancel windows.

The marsh was white where the silver rays caught the vapours that floated over it, and dark beyond that brilliant pathway; there was a track of light upon the sea. We stood a moment and looked. Even to me it seemed strange to leave the brightness of within for this weird, solemn brightness of the silent world without. I think I sighed. I really was very sorry now for having made that speech.

We walked round the terrace outside the chapel. We scarcely spoke five words. When we came to the wood that shades the chapel on the further side we stopped. The path that led into it lost itself in blackness.

"It's quite a place for ghosts, isn't it?" said I.

"Yes; it's not the place for any one else," laughed the Squire. "Any one less used to dampness would certainly catch their death of cold."

"Oh, you mustn't laugh at ghosts," answered I. "I believe in ghosts. And I'm sure this wood must be full of ghosts—so many wonderful people must have walked about in it hundreds of years ago."

"So long ago as that?" said he.

He was determined to treat my fancy lightly. But his laugh was kindly. We turned back to the white moonlight, but not before I had noticed a tall white figure in the black depths, which I should have been quite sure was a ghost if I had not been equally sure of the contrary. The figure was not alone. If it had been, I should have accosted it. As it was, I took the Squire's arm and walked away quickly in the direction of the house. The music had struck up again. The swing of an entrancing Strauss waltz came floating out on the night wind.

"We must go indoors," said the Squire, not at all like a man who was longing to dance to that lovely air; "I'm engaged for this to Miss Thorne."

Poor man! No doubt he had had nearly enough by that time of playing the host and of dancing every dance; he wanted a few minutes' rest.

I too was engaged, but not to a very delightful partner. After one turn round the room with him, I complained of the heat, and begged him to take me outside. Of course we went towards the ruin.

Of the few couples who had come out, all had gone that way, because from that point there was a break in the belt of trees, and one could see to the marsh and the sea. But we went round the chapel to the wood on the other side.

"I say, it looks gloomy in there, doesn't it?" said the young man at my side.

"Yes," answered I, but I was not looking into the wood now.

I had glanced into the interior of the ruin as we had passed, and I had seen a tall black figure leaning in the deep shadow against the side of the central arch that stood up so quietly against the soft sky. I felt quite sure that the "ghost" whom I had seen a few minutes before was close by. I was nearly certain that I saw a white streak that was not moonlight beyond the bend of the arch.

I turned round and went down the lawn a few steps, my companion following. He began to talk to me, but I did not know what he said. I was listening beyond him to another voice. It fell sadly upon my ear.

"I've no doubt the girl was right," it said. "I'm sure she was right. I had never noticed it before, but his leading you out to-night before every one was very significant."

It was my sister's voice that answered, but she must almost have whispered the words, for I could not hear them at all.

The man spoke again.

"Yes; that's not very likely," answered he, with a soft laugh. "Of course, how could he help it? Oh, I ought to have gone away," he added; "I ought to have gone away as soon as I had seen you. But I couldn't. You see even to-night, when I have tried to keep away from you, you have made me come to you at last. And I didn't think that I was doing you any harm till now."

He emphasised the word "you." I did not notice it then, but I recollect it now.

Again my sister's voice said something,—what, I could not hear.

"Do you mean that, dearest? do you mean that?" said he softly. "That you would not marry him if you could help it, although he would make such a lady of you? Ah, then I think I can guess something!"

A fiery blush rose to my cheek. I was glad that in the white moonlight my companion could not see it. I ran quickly down the slope of grass on to the gravel walk. It was dreadful, dreadful that I should have listened to these words which were meant for her ear alone.

"Come," I called to the lad, who loitered behind; "come, it's cold, we must go in."

He followed me slowly.

"I believe there were a man and a girl spooning behind that wall," he said, with a grin.

How I hated him! I have never spoken to him from that day to this, and yet, was it his fault?

We went back into the ball-room. The waltz was over. I had a partner for the last one, but I did not care to dance it. I was watching for Joyce, and when I saw her presently floating round with her hand on Captain Forrester's arm, I thought I was quite happy.

But mother was not happy. She had thought that Joyce would dance the last dance with Squire Broderick. She said that father was tired, and that she wanted to go. And indeed his face looked very weary, and his heavy lips heavier than ever.

No doubt we were all tired, for the Squire too had lost the cheerful look that he had worn all through the evening.

I sat and waited for Joyce, and I wondered to myself whether any one would ever make love to me with his heart in his voice.

CHAPTER XI.

TIME dragged heavily on my hands after the excitement of the Squire's ball was over. It was not only that I had to go back to the routine of everyday life—for there was still the concert to look forward to, which gave us plenty of interest—but it was that during a whole fortnight I had been looking for news from Joyce, and that Joyce had said never a word. No; she had rather been more silent than usual, constrained and unlike her own serene and happy self; and I had been frightened—frightened at sight of the torrent that I had let loose, and doubtful whether, in spite of all his democratic theories, this handsome, courtly, chivalrous knight, who was my embodiment of romance, was really a fit mate for the humble damsel nurtured in the quiet shade.

Well, anyhow the torrent rolled on, whether it was really I who had set it free or not, and I was forced to stand aside and watch its course without more ado.

There had been plenty to watch. The village concert had come and gone; it had taken place a week after the Squire's ball. Captain Forrester had worked us very hard for it towards the end. We had had practisings every afternoon, and I had rehearsed my solos indefatigably; but, save for singing in the glees and playing an accompaniment now and then, Joyce had taken no active part in the musical performance, and I had fancied that she had kept out of the way a great deal more than she need have done.

I could not understand her at all. She would not give Frank the ghost of a chance of saying a word to her alone; she shunned him as she shunned me.

On the night of the concert he was, of course, too much excited until the performance was over, to remember even Joyce at first; for he was one of those natures who throw themselves ardently into whatever they take up, and he was just as eager over this entertainment, of which he had accepted the responsibility, as though it were going to be given before a select company instead of before a handful of country bumpkins.

Well, he was rewarded for his pains. The concert was voted a brilliant success, and by a long way the best that had ever been given in the village.

"When quiet stars are in the skies," and "Robin Adair," which I sang "by request," as an *encore*, were greatly applauded, as were also the glees that we had so patiently practised ; and though, of course, the crowning point of the evening was Captain Forrester's own song, poured forth in his rich, mellow baritone, we had none of us reason to complain of the reception that we got ; and the stone walls of the old town hall, that had stood since the days when the headsman was still an institution, responded to the clapping of the people.

To be sure, they wanted father to stand up and give them a speech, but he would have nothing to do with that on this occasion : he said it was one of relaxation and not of work ; and he always refused to touch upon things that were sacred to him, for mere effect, or in anything but the most serious spirit. He wished them all good-night, and told them so.

I remember a curious incident that occurred that night. One of the American oil-lamps that lighted the hall took fire; a panic arose in the little crowd; the women pressed to the door. But Captain Forrester, calling out to the people in strong, reassuring tones to keep their seats, seized the lamp, carried it burning above the heads of the throng, and threw it down into the little courtyard without.

When the fright was over I missed father and Joyce. Him I found at once, sitting on the steps with two sobbing little ones on his knees—two little ones whose sisters had run out without them, and whose little hearts had been numbed with fear. Father would generally neglect any grown-up person in preference to a child. But Joyce I could not see.

I felt sure that she must have gone to look after Captain Forrester; but when presently he came back with his hand bandaged, and said that he had seen nothing of Joyce, I was really frightened. I discovered her sitting down in a dark corner of the courtyard, crying.

She said that she had been terrified by the accident, and had run out for safety before any one else. But her manner puzzled me. And for a whole week after that her manner continued to puzzle me.

Frank Forrester came every day to the Grange to see father. They had a new scheme on hand, an original scheme, a pet scheme of my dear father's—the scheme of all his schemes which he held most dear, and one which I know he had had for years, and had never dared hope would find favour with any one. It was a scheme for the succour of those poor children who had either no parents, or whose parents were anxious to get rid of them.

Of course, I did not understand the workings of it at the time, it not being possible that I should understand the requirements of the case; but from what I can recollect, gleaned from the scraps of talk that fell from father and Captain Forrester, I think it was intended to pick up cases which were not provided for in the ordinary foundling hospitals, and to rescue those poor wretched little creatures, whose parents were willing to part with them, from a life of sin and degradation.

The children were to be taught a trade, and were to be honourably placed in situations when they left the home.

Of course it was a vast scheme—how vast I am sure father cannot have grasped at the time; but although he must have had grave doubts of the possibility of its success, he was carried away for the moment by Frank Forrester's wild enthusiasm upon the subject, and was persuaded by him to try and put it into immediate practice.

I think he was more drawn to Frank than ever by this. I think he was drawn to every one who cared for children. But although the Captain was very enthusiastic over this scheme, he found time to look at Joyce and to sigh for a word from her, for a chance of seeing her alone, and she would not give it him.

For a whole fortnight after that memorable evening of the Squire's ball she had kept him sighing; at least, I think that she had, and I was very sorry for him.

To be sure, mother's eyes were vigilant — it needed some bravery to elude mother's eyes; but then I thought that, if one wanted a thing very much, one would be brave.

Was Joyce cold-hearted? Was that why her face was so calm and so beautiful?

But one day, at last, the Squire and his nephew came and went away together, and mother, thinking the visit was over for the day, had gone out on household errands. I was coming in from taking a parcel of poor linen to the Vicarage when Deborah met me in the hall.

"That there Captain's in with Miss Joyce in the parlour," said she. "They didn't want no light, they didn't. But I've took 'em in the lamp just this minute."

She said this with grim determination, and went off grumbling.

Deborah wanted Joyce to marry the Squire, and I fancy she suspected me of furthering her acquaintance with the Captain.

I did not go in as Deborah suggested, not until close upon the time when I was afraid mother would come home.

Joyce was sitting in the big arm-chair with her hands clasped across her knees, gazing into the fire.

Captain Forrester sat at the old spinet—our best new piano was in the front parlour—and touched its poor old clanging keys gently, and sang soft notes to it in his soft mellow voice. They were passionate love-songs, as I now know; but the words were in foreign tongues, and I did not understand them; no doubt Joyce did. He rose when I came in, and asked what o'clock it was.

I told him, and he laughed his gay, sympathetic laugh, and declared that at the Grange he never knew what the time was; he believed we kept our clocks all wrong. Then he said that he could not wait any longer for father that evening, but would come to see him in the morning. He went up to Joyce, and held out his hand. She shook herself, as though to rouse herself from a dream, and rose. This time it was no mistake of mine. Captain Forrester held Joyce's hand a long while.

"Good-bye—till to-morrow morning," said he, in a low voice.

She did not answer, and he turned to me.

"Good night, Miss Margaret," he said, and there was a ring in his voice — an impressiveness even towards me — which seemed to say that something particular had happened.

When he was gone, I felt that I must know what it was. This barrier of reserve between two sisters was ridiculous.

"Joyce," said I, half impatiently, "have you nothing to tell me?"

She looked up at me. A flush spread itself all over her neck and face, her short upper lip trembled a little,—it always did with any emotion.

"Yes," answered she simply. "Captain Forrester wants to marry me."

I did not reply. Now that it had come to this pass as I wished, I was frightened, as I have said.

But Joyce was looking up at me with an appealing look in her eyes. I stooped down and kissed her.

"You dear old thing," I said; "I'm so glad. I hoped he had,—I have hoped all along he would."

"I thought you wished it," she said, with childlike simplicity.

I laughed.

"Of course I knew from the very beginning that he would fall in love with you," I said.

"O Margaret, don't say that!" pleaded she. And then, after a pause, with a little sigh she added, "I should have thought he would have been wiser than to fall in love with a country girl, when there must be so many town girls who are better fitted to him."

"Nonsense!" cried I. "The woman who is fitted to a man is the woman whom he loves."

"Do you think so?" murmured she, diffidently.

"Why, of course," I cried, warming as I went on, and forgetting my own doubts in laughing at hers. "A man doesn't marry a woman for the number of languages that she speaks, and that kind of thing,—at least not a man like Captain Forrester. I don't know how you can misjudge him so. Don't you believe that he loves you?"

"Oh yes," she murmured again; "I think that he loves me."

I said no more for a while. Joyce's attitude puzzled me. That she should speak so diffidently of the adoration of a man who had addressed to her the passionate words which I had overheard, passed my comprehension.

I fell to wondering what was her feeling towards him. More than ever I felt that she had passed beyond me into a world of which I knew only in dreams. I had risen now, and stood over the fire.

"I always dreamt of something like that for you, Joyce," said I. "I always felt that you weren't a bit suited to marry a country bumpkin, but I never pictured to myself anything so good as this for you. Mother had grand ideas for you, I know. Oh yes; and you know she had now," added I, in answer to a deprecatory "Oh, don't!" from my sister. "But I should have hated what she wanted; and I don't believe you would ever have consented. But Captain Forrester is not a landed proprietor; he cares for the rights of the people, as father does. He is a fine fellow; and then he is young, and has never loved any one else," added I, dropping my voice.

I suppose I said this in allusion to the Squire's first wife.

She did not say anything, and I knelt down beside her. "Dear Joyce," I whispered—and I do believe my voice trembled—"I do want you to be happy. And though I shall feel dreadfully lonely when you have gone away and left me, I shan't be sorry, because I shall be so glad you have got what I wanted you to have."

She squeezed my hand very tight.

"Oh, but I shan't be married, dear, not for ever so long yet," said she. "Why, you forget, we don't know what father and mother will say."

"Why, father and mother can only want what is best for you," answered I. And I believed it.

Nevertheless, what father and mother, or at all events what mother thought best, was not what I thought best.

When Captain Forrester came the next morning, I knew before he passed into father's business-room that he was not going to receive a very satisfactory answer. He was expected; his answer was prepared, and I was to blame that it was.

That evening, after the Captain's proposal to Joyce, the Squire sent down a message to ask whether father would be disengaged, and if he were, whether he might come down after supper to smoke a pipe with him. We were seated around the meal when Deborah brought in the message.

"Certainly," answered father. "Say that I shall be pleased to see Mr Broderick." But when she was gone out, he added gruffly, "What the deuce can the Squire want to see me for? I don't know of anything that I need to talk to him about."

He looked at mother, but mother did not answer. She assumed her most dignified air, and there was a kind of suppressed smile on her face which irritated me unaccountably. As soon as the meal was over, she reminded us that we had the orange marmalade to tie up and label, and we were forced to leave her and father together.

I went very reluctantly, for I wanted to hear what they had to say, and Deborah was in a very inquisitive mood—asking us how it was that the Squire had not invited us up to supper at the Manor these three weeks, and when this fine gentleman from London was going to take himself back again to his own home.

I left Joyce to answer her, and found an excuse to get back again to the parlour as fast as I could. Father and mother sat opposite to one another in their high-backed chairs by the fire. Father had not been well since that night of the ball. I think he had caught a chill in the east wind, and was feeling his gout again a little. I think it must have been so, or he would scarcely have remained sitting. Knowing him as I did, I was surprised; for I knew by his face in a moment that he was in a bad temper, and he never remained sitting when he was in a bad temper.

"Nonsense, Mary, nonsense!" he was saying. "I'm surprised at a woman of your good sense running away with such ideas! Mere friendship, mere friendliness — that's all."

"Well," answered mother, stroking her

knee, over which she had turned up her dress to save it from scorching at the fire, "it was not only his taking Joyce out to dance first before all the county neighbours, but he took me in to supper himself—and, I can assure you, was most attentive to me."

"Well, and I should have expected nothing less of him," said father. "The man is a gentleman, and you have been a good friend to him. No man, squire or not, need be ashamed of taking my wife in to supper —no, not before ten counties!"

Mother smiled contentedly.

"Every one can't be expected to see as you do, Laban," said she. "I think it was done with a purpose."

"Oh! And, pray, what purpose?" asked father, in his most irritating and irritated tone.

Mother was judicious; perhaps even she was a little frightened. She did not answer just at first. I had slid behind the door of the jam-press in the corner of the room, and now I began putting the rows of marmalade pots in order. She had not noticed me.

"I think the Squire wishes to marry our eldest daughter," said she slowly; and then she reached down her knitting from the mantel-piece and began to ply her needles.

There was a dreadful silence for a minute.

"I have thought so for a long time," added mother. "I have felt sure that he must have some other reason for coming here so often beside mere friendship for two old people."

Father leant forward in his chair, resting his head on the arm of it, as though about to rise, but not rising.

"Well, then, if he has any other reason, the longer he keeps it to himself the better," said he, in a voice that he tried to prevent from becoming loud. "But we have no right to judge him until we know," added he. "You've made a mistake, mother. The Squire isn't thinking of marrying again. He's no such fool."

"I don't see that he'd be such a fool to wish to marry a sweet girl that he has known all his life," remonstrated mother.

"He can marry no girl of mine—at least, not with my consent," declared father loudly, his temper getting the better of him. "My girls must marry in their own rank of life, or not at all. I have no need of the gentry to put new blood into our veins. We are good enough and strong enough for ourselves, any day. But come, old lady, come," he added more softly, trying to recover himself, "you've made a mistake. It's very natural. Mothers will be proud of their children, and women must always needs fancy riches and honours are the best things in the world."

"Oh, I don't fancy that, I'm sure, Laban," answered mother. "But I can't think you would really refuse such a true and honest man for Joyce."

"Well, then, Mary, look here; you be quite sure that I shall never consent to my daughter marrying a man who must come down a peg in the eyes of the world to wed her," began he, raising his voice again, and speaking very slowly.

He looked mother keenly in the face, but he got no further than that, for I emerged from the jam-cupboard with a pot in my hand; and at the same moment Deborah flung open the door and announced Squire Broderick. Mother put down her skirt quickly, and father sank back in his chair. There was an anxious look upon the Squire's face which puzzled me, but he tried to laugh and look like himself as he shook hands with us.

"You mustn't speak so loud, Maliphant, you mustn't speak so loud if you want to keep things a secret," laughed he. "Marrying? Who is going to be married, if you please?"

Mother blushed, and even father looked uncomfortable.

"We were only talking of possibilities, Squire, very remote possibilities," said he. "The women are fond of taking time by the forelock in such matters, you know. But now we'll give over such nonsense, and bring our minds to something more sensible. You wanted to see me?"

"Yes," answered the Squire. "And I have only a few minutes. My nephew leaves to-morrow, and we have some little affairs to attend to."

"Your nephew leaves to-morrow!" cried I aghast. They all turned round and looked at me, and I felt myself blush.

"He never said so when he was here this afternoon," I added hurriedly, with a little nervous laugh.

"No, I don't suppose he knew it when we were here," answered the Squire, evidently ignorant of the Captain's second visit alone. "He had a telegram from his mother this evening, begging him to return home at once."

I said no more, and Squire Broderick turned to father. "Can you give me a few minutes?" asked he.

Father rose. It vexed me to see that he rose with some difficulty. He was evidently sadly stiff again, and it vexed me that the Squire should see it. Without uttering a word he led the way to his business-room.

I remained where I was, with the jam-pot in my hand, looking at mother, who sat by the fire knitting. There was a little smile upon her lips that annoyed me immensely.

"I think I ought to tell you, mother, that I was behind the jam-cupboard door while you and father were talking, and that I heard what you said," said I, suddenly."

"Well, of course I did not expect you to come intruding where you were not wanted, Margaret," said mother; "but I don't know that it matters. I'm not ashamed of what I said."

"Of course not," answered I; "and I've guessed you had that notion in your head these months past."

"I don't know, I'm sure, what business you had to guess," said mother. "It wasn't your place, that I can see."

"And I may as well tell you that I'm quite sure Joyce would never think of the Squire if he did want to marry her," continued I, without paying any attention to this remark. I paused a moment before I added—"she couldn't, anyhow, because she's in love with another man."

Mother looked at me over her spectacles. She looked at me as though she did not see me, and yet she looked me through and through.

"Margaret," said she at last, loftily, "I consider it most unseemly of you to say such a thing of your sister. A well-brought-up girl don't go about falling in love with men in that kind of way."

"A girl must fall in love with the man she means to marry, mother; at least, so I should think," said I.

And I marched off into the kitchen with

the jam-pot that wanted a label, and did not come out again till I heard the business-room door open, and the Squire's voice in the hall.

"Well, you'll come to dinner on Thursday, anyhow, and see him," he was saying; "it need bind you to nothing."

Father grumbled something as he hobbled across, and I noticed again how lame he was that day. The Squire, seeing mother upon the threshold of the parlour door, stopped and added pleasantly, "Maliphant has promised to bring you up to dine at the Manor, so mind you hold him to his word." Mother assured him that she would, and the Squire went out.

"Well?" asked she, turning to father with a questioning look on her face, which was neither so hopeful nor so happy as it had been ten minutes ago.

"Well?" echoed he, somewhat crossly. Then his frown changing to a smile, he patted her on the arm, and said merrily, "No, mother, no. Wrong this time; wrong, old lady, upon my soul. The time hasn't come yet when we are to have the honour of having our daughters asked in marriage by the gentry."

"Hush, Laban, hush," cried mother, vexed; for the kitchen door stood open, and Joyce was within earshot. And then, following him into the parlour, whither I had already found my way, she added, "Maybe I'm not quite such a fool as you think, and the time will come one day, although it's not ripe just yet."

"A fool! Who ever called you a fool, Mary? Not I, I'm sure," declared father. "No, you're a true, shrewd woman, and, as you are generally right in such matters, I daresay you may prove right now: but all I want to make clear to you is, that whatever time the Squire's question comes—if it be a question of that nature—his answer will always be the same."

Mother said no more. She was a wise woman, and never pursued a vexed question when there was no need to do so. I, who was not so wise, thought that I now saw a fitting opportunity for putting in my own peculiar oar amid the troubled waters.

"I don't think you need trouble your head about it, father," I said. "Joyce will never marry Squire Broderick, even if he were to ask her. She's in love with Captain Forrester."

Father turned round with the pipe he was filling 'twixt his finger and thumb and looked at me.

"Margaret," said mother, "didn't I tell you just now that that was a most strange and unseemly thing to say?"

I did not answer, and father still looked at me with the pipe between his finger and thumb.

"In love with Captain Forrester, indeed!" continued mother scornfully. "And pray, how do you know that Captain Forrester is in love with Joyce?"

"Well, of course," answered I with a toss of my head, "girls don't fall in love with men unless the men are in love with them first. Who ever heard of such a thing? Of course he's in love with Joyce."

"Stuff and nonsense!" said mother emphatically, tapping the floor with her foot as she was wont to do when she was annoyed. "Captain Forrester and your sister haven't met more than half-a-dozen times in the course of their lives. I wonder what a love is going to be like that takes the world by storm after three weeks' acquaintance."

"There is such a thing as love at first sight," answered I, with what I know must have been an annoyingly superior air. It did not impress mother.

"A wondrous fine thing, I've been told," was all that she said.

I turned to father, who had not spoken. "Well, anyhow they're in love with one another," I repeated. "I know it as a fact, and he's coming here to-morrow morning to ask your leave to marry her."

"The devil he is!" ejaculated father, roused at last.

Mother dropped her knitting. I do believe her face grew white with horror.

"I always thought, Laban, it was a pity to have that young man about so much when we had grown-up girls at home," moaned she, quite forgetting my presence. "But you always would be so sure he was thinking of nothing but those politics of yours."

"To be sure, to be sure," murmured father.

"And he was always so pleasant to all of us," she went on, as though that too were something to deplore in him; "but I never did think he'd be wanting to marry a farmer's daughter. And I should like to know what he has got to marry any one upon?" added she after a pause, turning to me indignantly, as though I knew the Captain's affairs any better than she did.

"His captain's pay," answered I glibly, although I had been chilled for a moment by this remark. "And why should you consider him a ne'er-do-well, because he earns his living in a different way to what you do? He kills the country's enemies, and you till the country's land. They are both honourable professions by which a man gets his bread by the sweat of his brow."

I looked at father: all through I had spoken only to him. He smiled, and began to light his pipe. It was a sign that his mind was made up. Which way was it made up?

"Joyce is just the girl men do fall in love with," said I, wisely; "and as for her—well, you can't be surprised at her falling in love with a man whom you like so much yourself."

"Ay, I do like the young man," agreed father staunchly. "I can't help it. They're precious few such as he whose heads are full of aught but seeking after their own pleasure."

"Well, if you like him so much, why are you sorry that he wants to marry Joyce?" asked I, boldly.

"I did not say that I was sorry, lass," said father calmly.

My heart throbbed with pleasant triumph, but the battle was not over yet.

"Well, Laban, I don't suppose you can say that you're glad," put in mother almost tartly, "after what I've heard you say about girls marrying out of their own class in life."

"Captain Forrester is not rich and idle," said I.

"No!" answered mother scornfully, "he is not rich—you're right enough there; but he is a good sight more idle than many men who can afford to keep a wife in comfort. I know your sort of play soldiers that never see an enemy."

"He's rich enough for a girl of mine," replied father. "As to his being idle, I hope maybe he's going to do better work saving the lives of innocent children than he could have done slashing at what are called the nation's foes."

"Yes, yes," said mother, a trifle impatiently. "I make no doubt you're right. I've nothing against the young man, but I can't believe, Laban, as you really mean to say that you'd give your girl to him willingly."

"Well," answered father, "I'm bound to say I'm surprised at the news. But we old folk are apt to forget that we were young once,—and when I was a lad I loved you, Mary, so we mustn't be hard on the young ones. It's neither poverty nor riches, nor this nor that, as makes happiness—it's just love; and if the two love one another, we durstn't interfere."

"I don't understand you, Laban, indeed I don't," cried poor mother, beside herself with anxiety. "It's not according to what you were saying a few minutes ago, and you can't say it is."

Father was silent. I suppose he could

not help knowing in his heart that the objections to Captain Forrester must be practically the same as those to Squire Broderick, with the additional one that he was almost a stranger to us. But his natural liking for the young man obscured his vision to plain facts. Father and I were very much alike; what we wanted to be must be. But when I look back at that point in our lives, I pity poor mother, who was really the wisest and the most practical of us all.

"Well, mother, the lass must decide for herself," said father. "She's of age; she should know her own mind."

"Joyce knows her own mind well enough," said I. "She has told Frank Forrester that she will marry him, subject to your approval."

"I wonder she took the trouble to add so much as that," said mother at last. "Young folk nowadays have grown so clever, they seem to teach us old folk."

There was a tremor in her voice, and father rose and went across to her, laying his hand on her shoulder.

"Meg, go and tell your sister to come

here," said he in a moment. " You need not come back."

I was hurt at the dismissal, and I waited in the passage till Joyce came out from the interview; but her face was very white, and all that she would say was, "O Margaret, let them settle it. I don't want to have any will of my own."

I was very much disappointed, and was fain to be agreeably surprised, when on the following morning I heard that, after mature deliberation, our parents had decided to allow the Captain a year's probation.

I had been afraid that mother would entirely override all father's arguments: she generally did.

The affair was not to be called an engagement,—both were to be perfectly free to choose again; but if at the end of that time both were of the same mind, the betrothal should be formally made and announced.

Mother must, however, have been very hard in her terms; for the young folk were neither to meet nor to write to one another, nor to have any news of one another beyond what might transpire in the correspondence that father would be carrying on with Frank on outside matters.

Frank told me the conditions out in the garden, when I caught hold of him as he came out of father's study. The whole matter was to be a complete secret, shut closely within our own family. This mother repeated to me afterwards—I guessed very well with what intent. But although Frank must have suspected a possible rival in his uncle, he absolutely refused to be cast down.

The thought even crossed my mind that I should have liked my lover to have been a little more cast down. But no doubt he felt too sure of himself, even after the slight shock of surprise that it must have been to him to find his suit not at once accepted.

Nevertheless, as he passed out of the room where he had taken leave of Joyce alone, he bent forward towards me as I stood in the hall, and said gravely, "Miss Margaret, I trust her to you. Don't let her forget me."

My heart ached for him, and from that

moment it was afire with the steadfast resolve to support my sister's failing spirits, and preserve for her the beautiful romance which had so unexpectedly opened out before her.

CHAPTER XII.

Joyce and I sat in the apple-orchard one May afternoon. It was not often we sat idle; but Joyce was going away on the morrow on a visit to Sydenham, and we wanted a few minutes' quiet together.

There was no quiet indoors: mother was in one of her restless moods, and Mr Hoad was with father. I supposed he was still harping on that subject of the elections, for I could not tell why else he should come so often; but I could have told him that he might have spared his pains, for that father never altered his mind.

However, on this particular occasion I was glad that he came, for I thought that it might save father from missing Frank too much—although, to be sure, they did not seem to get on so well as before Frank's coming ; and I fancied that there was even the suspicion of a cloud on father's face when he closed the door after his man of business.

Who could wonder ? Who would like Hoad after Frank Forrester ? For my own part, I always avoided him, and that was why I had taken Joyce out of doors.

An east wind blew from the sea, and the marsh was bleak, though the lengthening shadows lay in soft tones across its crude spring greenness. The sun shone, and the thorn-trees that were abloom by the dykes made white spots along their straightness— softer memories of the snow that had so lately vanished, kindly promise of spring to come. Under the apple-trees heavy with blossom, the air was blue above the vivid emerald of the springing grass, and all around us slenderly sturdy grey trunks and angular boughs, softened by a wealth of rose-flushed flower, made delicate patterns upon the sky or against the glittering sea-line beyond the marsh.

But a spring scene with its frank, passionless beauty, its tenderness that is all promise and no experience, its arrogance of coming life, does sometimes put one out of heart with one's self, I think—although it should not have had that effect on one who stood in the same relation to life as did the spring to the year. Anyhow, I was not in my most cheerful frame of mind that day—not quite so arrogant and sanguine myself as was my wont.

Since the day when Captain Forrester had left the village three weeks ago, things had not gone to my liking. In the first place, I was not satisfied with this engagement of a year's standing, that was to be kept a profound secret from every one around. I thought it was not fair to Joyce. And then, and alas! I fear an even more active cause in my depression of spirits—Mr Trayton Harrod had been engaged as bailiff to Knellestone farm!

Yes; never should I have expected it. It was too horrible, but it was true. Father and mother had gone up to meet him at dinner at the Manor two days after the Captain's departure, and father had been forced to confess that he was a quiet, sensible, straightforward fellow, without any nonsense about him, and that there was no doubt that he knew what he was about.

It was very mortifying to me to hear father speak of him in that way, when I had quite made up my mind that he was sure not to know what he was about. But it seems that I was curiously mistaken upon this point.

Far from being a mere amateur at the business, he had been carefully educated for it at the Agricultural College at Ashford. His father had been of opinion that his own ventures had failed because of a too superficial knowledge of the subject—a knowledge only derived from natural mother-wit and practical observation—and he wished his son to labour under no such disadvantages.

I fancy Mr Harrod's father had been, as the country folk say, "a cut above his neighbours" in culture and social standing, and had taken to farming as a speculation when other things had failed. But of course this was no reason why his son should not make a good farmer, since he had been carefully educated to the business.

He was not wanting in practical experience

either. He had done all he could to retrieve the fortunes of his father's farm, but the speculation was too far gone before he took the reins; and the elder Harrod had died a ruined man, leaving his son to shift for himself.

All this I had gleaned from talk between my parents and the Squire in our own house; but it was mortifying, even though I had not guessed at that time that there was any real danger of his coming to Knellestone. For that had only been settled two days ago, and I could not help fancying that Mr Hoad was partly to blame.

Of course there was no denying that father had been ill again—not so seriously ill as in the winter, but incapacitated for active life. He had not been able to mount his horse nor to walk farther than the garden-plot at the top of the terrace for over a fortnight.

The doctor had suggested a bath-chair; but the idea of a farmer being seen in a bath-chair was positively insulting, and I would rather have seen him shut indoors for a month than showing himself to the neighbours in such a plight. The idea was abandoned; but gradually, and without any sign, his mind came round to the plan which he had at first so violently repudiated—that of a bailiff for Knellestone.

I do not know whether it was really Mr Hoad who had anything to do with his decision. He certainly had influence over father, and had been very often at the Grange of late, but it may have been merely the effect which Mr Harrod himself produced. Anyhow, a fortnight or so after the dinner at the Manor, father announced to us abruptly at the dinner-table that he had that morning written to engage " that young man of the Squire's" to come to Knellestone. His manner had been so queer when he said it, that nobody had questioned him further on the matter; and as for me, I had been so thoroughly knocked down by the news, that I do not think I had spoken to father since!

If my sister's departure had not been arranged—and in a great measure arranged by me—before this news had come, I am sure that I should not have suggested it; for it was the first time in our lives that we had been parted, and, reserved as I was, I felt that I wanted Joyce to be there during this family crisis.

She at least never allowed herself to be ruffled, and though this characteristic had its annoying side, there was comfort in it; and just at that particular moment we needed a soother, for the family was altogether in a somewhat ruffled condition.

Father was cross because of what he had been driven into doing with regard to the bailiff. Mother was cross because the Squire had not proposed for Joyce, and Captain Forrester had. And I was cross—more cross than any one—because I was an opinionated young woman, and wanted to have a finger in the management of every pie.

It was a good thing that Joyce took even her own share in these matters more quietly than I took it for her. Nevertheless even she was a little dismal that evening. How was it possible that she could be happy parted, without even the solace of correspondence, from the man whom she loved? I believe in my secret soul I set Joyce down as wanting in feeling for not fretting more than she did; but she *was* out of spirits, and mother had agreed with me that Joyce was pale, and had better choose this time for a visit to Aunt Naomi, which had been a promise for a long time. And now it was impossible to put it off.

Joyce came back from a dream with a little sigh, and turned towards me.

"Well, did you see Mr Trayton Harrod this morning, Margaret?" asked she. "Deborah says he was here to see father. When does he come for good?"

"I don't know, answered I shortly. "I know nothing at all about Mr Trayton Harrod."

Joyce sighed a little. "Deborah says he is a plain kind of man," continued she—"very tall and broad, and very short in his manners."

"He can't be too short in his manner for me," answered I. "He'll find me short too."

Joyce stretched out her hand and laid it on mine. It was a great deal for her to do. In the first place, we were not given to outward demonstrations of affection; and in the second place, Joyce knew that I abhorred sympathy, and that from my earliest childhood I had always hit out at people who dared to pity me for my hurts.

"Dear Margaret," said she, "I want you not to be so much set against this young man. Father said he was a straightforward, good sort of fellow, you know; and you can't be sure that he will be disagreeable until you know him."

"I don't suppose he is going to be disagreeable at all," declared I. "He may be the most delightful man in the world—I've no doubt he is. I only say that he is nothing to me. I shall have nothing to do with him, and I shan't know whether he is delightful or not."

"Well, if you begin like that, it *will* be setting yourself against him," said Joyce bravely. She paused a moment, and then added, "I'm in hopes it will be a good thing for father. I've often thought of late that the work was too hard for him. Father's not the man he was."

"Father's all right," insisted I. "It's always the strongest men who have the gout. You'll see father will walk the young ones off the ground yet when it comes to a day's work. A man can work for his own,—he works whether he be tired or not; but a hireling—why should a hireling work when he hasn't a mind to? It's nothing to him; he gets his wage any way."

This theory seemed to trouble Joyce a bit, for she was silent.

"No," said I, "it'll be no go. He won't understand anything at all about it, and all he will do will be to set everybody by the ears."

"I don't see why that need be," persisted Joyce. "The Squire says that he has been brought up to hard work, and that he has quite a remarkable knowledge of the country."

"Yes, what good did his knowledge of the country do him?" asked I, scornfully. "He managed his father's farm in Kent, and his father died a bankrupt. I don't call that much of a recommendation."

I had been obliged to come down from my high horse as to this friend of the Squire's being one of his own class, an impoverished gentleman who wanted a living, for there was no doubt that he had been born and bred on a farm, and had been, moreover, specially educated to his work; but I had managed to find out something else in his disfavour nevertheless.

My sister was puzzled as to how to answer this. "I did not know that that was so," said she.

"Of course it is so," repeated I. "That's why he must needs take a job."

"Poor fellow!" murmured Joyce.

"Nonsense!" cried I. "He ought to have been able to save the farm from ruin. It's no good pitying people for the misfortunes they bring upon themselves. The weak always go to the wall."

I did myself injustice with this speech. It did not really express my feelings at all, but my temper was up.

Joyce looked pained. "Perhaps the affairs of the farm were too bad to be set right before he took up the management," suggested she. "At all events, I suppose father knows best."

"I can't understand father," exclaimed I hastily. "He seems to me to take much more interest in plans for saving pauper children than he does in working his own land."

"O Margaret! how can you say such a

thing," cried Joyce aghast. "You know that father is often laid by, and unable to go round the farm."

"Yes, yes, I know," I hastened to answer, ashamed of my outburst, and remembering that I was flatly contradicting what I had said two minutes before. "Nobody really has the interest in the place that father has, of course. That's why I don't want him to take a paid bailiff. When he is laid by, he can manage it through me."

"I'm afraid that never answers," said Joyce, shaking her head; "I'm afraid business matters need a man. People always seem to take advantage of a woman."

I tried to laugh. "I wonder what Deborah would say to that," I said, trying to turn the matter into a joke.

"Deborah doesn't attempt anything out of her own province," answered Joyce.

It was another of her quiet home-thrusts. She little guessed how they hurt, or she would never have dealt them,—she who could not bear to hurt a fly.

"Margaret," began she again, her mind still set on that conciliatory project which she had undertaken, "do promise me one thing before I go. I don't like going away, and it makes me worse to think you will be working yourself up into a fever of annoyance at what can't be helped. Do promise me that you won't begin by being set against the young man. It'll make it very uncomfortable for everybody if you are, and you won't be any the happier. You can be so nice when you like."

I looked at her surprised. It was so very rarely that Joyce came out of her shell to take this kind of line. It showed it must have been working in her mind for long.

"Yes, dear, yes," said I, really touched by her anxiety, "I'll try and be nice."

"You do take things so hard," continued she, "and it's no use taking things hard. Now if you liked you might help father still, with Mr Harrod, and he might be quite a pleasant addition to your life."

"That's ridiculous, Joyce," I answered sharply. "You must see that he and I could never be friends. All I can promise is not to make it harder for him to settle down amongst the folk, for it'll be hard enough. However clever the Squire may think him, he won't understand this country, nor this weather, nor these people at first, — there's no doubt of that. He'll make lots of mistakes. But there, for pity's sake don't let's talk any more about him," cried I, hastily. "I'm sick of the man; and on our last evening too, when I've such a lot to say to you."

"What have you to say to me?" asked my sister, looking round suddenly, and with an uneasy look in her face.

"Oh, come, you needn't look like that," laughed I. "It's nothing horrid like you have been saying to me. It's about Captain Forrester."

Her face grew none the less grave. "What about him?" asked she in a low voice.

"Well, I'm going to fight for you, Joyce, while you're away," said I. "I don't think you've been over-pleased about having to go to Aunt Naomi, and perhaps you have owed me a grudge for having had a finger in settling it. It will be dull for you boxed up with the old lady and her rheumatism, but you must bear in mind that I shall be working for you here, better than, maybe, I could if you were by."

"Why, Meg, what do you want to do?" asked my sister aghast.

"I'm going to get mother to make your engagement shorter," said I, getting up and standing in front of her, "and I'm going to make her allow you and Frank to write to one another."

"O Meg, how can you?" gasped Joyce.

"Well, I'm going to," repeated I, doggedly. She did not reply. She clasped her hands in her lap with a nervous movement, and dropped her eyes upon them.

"Mother said that the year's engagement was so that you and Captain Forrester should learn to be quite sure of yourselves. Now, how are you to be any surer of yourselves than you are now if you don't get to know one another any better? And how are you going to know one another any better if you never see one another, and never write to one another?"

Joyce paused before she replied. She lifted her eyes and fixed them on the channel, of which the long tortuous curves, winding across the marsh to the sea, were blue now with an opaque colour in the growing greyness of the evening.

"Perhaps mother don't wish us to know one another any better. Perhaps she wishes us to forget one another," said she at last, slowly.

"I know mother wants you to forget one another, because she wants you to marry the Squire," said I bluntly, "but father doesn't."

"O Meg, don't," whispered Joyce.

"Well, of course you know it," laughed I, a little ashamed of myself, "and you know that I know it. But you never would have married him, dear, so mother is none the worse off if you marry Captain Forrester, and you are not going to forget him because they want you to."

"No," murmured she. "But oh, Meg," she added, hastily rising too, and taking my hand, "I don't want you to say anything to them about it. It's settled now, and it's far best as it is. I had far rather let it be, and take my chance."

"What do you mean by taking your chance?" cried I. "You mean to say that you can trust to your lover not to forget you? Well, I suppose you can. He worships you, and I suppose one may fairly expect even a man to be faithful one little year. But, meanwhile, you will both of you be unhappy instead of being comparatively happy, as you would be if you could write to one another and see one another sometimes. Now that seems to me to be useless, and I don't see why it need be. At all events, I shall try to prevent it."

"You're a good, faithful old Meg, as true as steel," said Joyce tenderly, taking my hand; "and I suppose you can't understand how I feel, because we are so different. But I want you to believe that I would much rather wait. Indeed I would much rather wait."

I gazed at her in silence. Once more there stole over me a strange feeling of awe, born of the conviction that Joyce had floated slowly away from me on the bosom of a stream that was to me unknown. Whither did it lead, and what was it like? What was this "being in love," of which I had dreamed of late—for her if not for myself? I laughed constrainedly.

"Well, I never was in love," said I, "and perhaps I never shall be. But I feel pretty sure that when a girl loves a man and he loves her, being parted must be like going about without a piece of one's own self. No, Joyce, you can't deceive me. I know that you want to see him every hour and every minute of your life, and that, when you don't, something goes wrong inside you all the while."

Joyce sighed gently, and drew her shawl around her. "You're so impetuous," sighed she. "Liking one person doesn't make one forget every one else."

"*Liking!*—no," said I, and then I stopped.

The marsh-land had grown dark with a passing cloud, and the aspens on the cliff shivered in the rising wind. A window opened in the house behind, and Deborah's voice came calling to us across the lawn.

"Well, whatever you two must needs go catching your deaths of cold out there for, I don't know," cried she, as we came up to her. "And not so much as a young man to keep you company! Oh! there's two dismal faces," laughed she, as I pushed past her.

"Well, I was wiser in my time. The men never gave me no thoughts, good nor bad."

"No, you never got any one to mind you then as Reuben minds you now," cried I.

But Joyce stopped the retort by asking what we were wanted for.

"There's company in the parlour," answered she, speaking to me still. "The Squire's come to bid Miss Joyce good-bye, and there's your friend Mr Hoad."

I made no answer to this thrust, but as we passed through the passage, the door of father's room opened, and the voice of Mr Hoad said, with a laugh, "No, I'm afraid you will never get any good out of him. A brilliant talker, a charming fellow, but no backbone in him. I was deceived in him myself at first, but he's no go. I should think the less any one reckoned on him for anything the better."

"You don't understand him," began father warmly; but he stopped, seeing us.

My cheeks flushed with anger. There was a grin on Deborah's face, but my sister's was serene.

She could not have understood.

CHAPTER XIII.

JOYCE had been gone a week before Mr Trayton Harrod arrived. I had preserved my gloomy silence on the subject of his coming, although I was dying to know all about it; and as father had given in to my mood by telling me no particulars, it so happened that I did not even know the exact day of his arrival.

It was a Monday, and baking day. There was plenty to do, now that Joyce was gone, and I did not do her work as she did it. Mother was constantly reminding me of the fact. It did not make me do the work any quicker, or like doing it any better; but, of course, it was natural that mother should see the difference, and remark on it.

At last, however, the baking and mending and dusting was all done, and mother gave me leave to take a little basket of victuals to an old couple who lived down by the sea. I had been very miserable, feeling pitiably how little I had done at present towards fulfilling my promise to Joyce of trying to make things pleasant, and sadly conscious that I was not in mother's good books, or, for that matter, in father's either, for which I am afraid I cared more. He had scarcely spoken a word to me all the week.

Poor father! Why did I not remember that it was far worse for him than it was for me? But as I ran across the lawn, with Taff yelping at my heels, I do not believe that I gave a thought to his anxieties, although I must have seen his dear old head bending over the farm account-books through the study window as I passed. I was so glad to have done with the housekeeping, that I forgot everything else in the tender sunshine of a May afternoon that was flecking the marsh with spots of light, shifting as the soft clouds shifted upon the blue sky. How could any troubles matter, either my own or other people's, when there was a chance of being within scent of the sea-weed and within taste of the salt sea-brine?

I whistled the St Bernard, and we set off on a race down the cliff. My hat flew off, I caught it by the strings; all the thickness of my hair uncoiled itself and rippled down my back. I felt the hairpins tumble out one by one, and knew that a great curly red mass must be floating in the wind; but I had a hundred yards to run yet before I came to the elms at the foot of the hill—and Taff was hard to beat.

Alongside the runnels that hemmed the lane, a riband, bluer than the sea or sky, ran bordering the green; it was made up of thousands of delicate veronica blossoms, opening merry eyes to the sun, and the red campion dotted the bank under the cliff, and the cuckoo-flowers nodded their pale clusters on edges of little dykes. But I did not see the flowers just then. I ran on and on, jumping the gate that divides the marsh from the road almost as Taffy jumped it himself—on and on along the dyke, without stopping, till I came to the first thorn-tree that grows upon the bank; and there, at last, I was fain to throw myself down to rest, out of breath and trembling.

What a run it was! I remember it to this day. It drove away all my ill-temper; and as I sat there twisting up my hair again, and laughing at Taff, who understood the joke just as if he were a human being, I had no more thought of anything ajar than had the white May trees that dotted the marsh all along the brown banks of the dykes, and lay so harmoniously against the faint blue of the sky, where it sank into the deeper blue of the sea beyond.

Dimly, beyond the flaken stretch of plain that was slowly flushing with the growing green, one could see the little waves rippling out across the yellow sands, with the sunlight flashing upon their crests; over the meadows red and white cattle wandered, and little spotless lambs played with their mothers on the fresher banks; tufts of tender primroses grew close to my hand, fish leapt in the still grey waters of the dyke, birds sang in the belt of trees under the Manor-house, lapwing made strange bleating and chirping sounds amid the newly sprouting growth of the rushes that mingled softly with the faint gold of last year's mown crop: the cuckoo's note came now and then through the air. The spring had come at last.

I tied on my hat again and jumped up. I began to sing, too, as I walked. I was merry. What with Captain Forrester, and what with the trouble about the bailiff, and what with Joyce's departure, and the household duties falling upon me, I had not been out among my favourite haunts for a long time, and the sight of the birds and the beasts and the flowers was new life to me. I noted the marks of the year's growth as only one notes them who knows the country by heart: I knew that the young rooks were already on the wing, that the swifts and the swallows had built their nests, that the song-thrush was hatching her brood, and that a hunt along the sunny sandy banks under the lee of the hill would discover the round holes where the little sand-martin would be laboriously scooping her nest some two feet deep into the soft ground.

I promised myself a happy afternoon when next I should have leisure, searching for plover's eggs along the banks of the dykes where the moor-hen and lapwing make their homes; but to-day I dared not loiter, for the old couple for whom I was bound lived under the shadow of the great rock where the marsh ends and the land swells up into white chalk cliffs fronting the sea, and that was four good miles from where I now was. Taff and I put our best legs foremost, vaulting the gates that separated the fields, and crossing the white bridges over the water, until at last we came to where the dyke meets the sea, and the martello towers stud the coast.

I confess we had not always walked quite straight. Once my attention had been caught by the hovering of a titlark in the vicinity of a bank by the wayside, and I had not been able to resist the temptation of climbing a somewhat perilous ascent to look for the nest, whose neighbourhood I guessed. It was on the face of a curious sort of cliff that lay across the marsh : one side of it sloped down into the pasture-land, but the other presented a grey rugged front to the greensward below, and told of days when the sea must have lapped about its massive sides, and eaten its way into the curious caves where now young oaks and mountain-ash clove to the barren soil.

About half-way up the nethermost bank of this cliff I found the nest of the titlark beneath a heather bush. But in it sat a young cuckoo alone and scarcely fledged, while lying down the bank, about a foot from the margin of the nest, lay the two little nestlings of the parent bird. I picked them up and warmed them in my hand, and put them back in the nest, where they soon lifted their heads again. Then I stood a moment and watched. The young cuckoo began struggling about till it got its back under one of them, and, blind as it still was, hitched it up to the open part of the nest, and shoved it out on to the bank. Once more I picked the poor little bird up and put it back into its mother's nest. Then seeing that the cruel little interloper seemed to have made up its mind to try no more ejecting for the moment, I slid down the bank again and went on, promising myself, however, to look in upon this quarrelsome family on my way home.

This little adventure delayed us, but we

ran a great part of the remainder of the way to make up for it, and reached old Warren's cottage somewhat out of breath, and I with red cheeks and hair sorely dishevelled by the journey. However, as we were old friends, we were soon restored by the kindly welcome that we got. Taffy lay down on the hearth with the great Persian cat, and I took my seat in the chimney-corner, Mrs Warren insisting on preferring the bed for a seat.

It was a funny little hut, nestled away under the shadow of the towering cliff, with the sea lapping or roaring within fifty yards of it, and the lonely marsh stretching away miles and miles to the right of it. No one knew why Warren had built it, but some fancied that he still had smuggled goods hidden away in the caves of the cliffs, and if so, he naturally chose a dwelling-place hard by, and not too much under the eye of man. It was a poor hovel, better to die in than to live in, one would have thought; but old Warren seemed to be of a contented disposition, and to enjoy his life well enough, although as much could not apparently be said of his wives, of whom he had had three already. The present one had lasted the longest, the former two having been killed off in comparatively early life (according to Warren) by the loneliness of their life and the terrors of the elements which they had witnessed.

Warren was a dramatic old fellow, and could tell many a story of shipwreck and disaster, and even (when pressed) of encounters between the revenue cutters and the smugglers' boats, of dangerous landings on this dangerous bit of coast, and of nights when it was all the "boys" could do to get their kegs of spirits safely ashore and buried in the sand before morning. This afternoon he was in particularly good spirits. Something in the colour of the land and the sea, and in the direction of the wind, had reminded him of a day when the fog had come up suddenly and had caused disaster, although, to my eye, the heavens were clear and fair as any one could wish. I soon drew from him the account of a terrible struggle between the Government officers and the smugglers, when the fog had given the latter a miraculous and unexpected triumph, and this led on to the tale — oft-repeated but never stale—of the wreck of the Portuguese "merchant," when the "lads" picked up the wicker bottles that floated ashore, and drank themselves sick with eau-de-Cologne in mistake for brandy.

This was my favourite story; but it was hard to know whether to laugh or to cry when Mrs Warren number three would shake her head sympathetically at the tearful account of the demise of Mrs Warren number two, who "lay a-dying within, while the lads drank the spirit without," and old Warren was forced to take a drain himself to help him in his trouble.

The time always passed quickly for me with the funny old couple in their funny old hovel under the cliff, and it was late afternoon before I got out again on to the beach. Warren's memories had not been awakened by mere fancy; his prophecy was right. There was a heavy sea-fog over the marsh, blown up by a wind from the east. I gathered my cloak around me, and set off walking as fast as I could. The mist was so thick that the dog shook himself as he ran on in front of me; the damp stood in great drops on the bristles of his shaggy coat and of my rough homespun cloak; it took the curl even out of my curly hair, which hung down in dank masses by the side of my face.

I could not see the sea, though I could hear it lapping on the shore close by: I could not even see the dyke at my left, and yet it was not thirty yards away. I knew the way well enough, however, and the fog only made an amusing variety to an everyday walk. I started off merrily, avoiding the road, which was not the shortest way, and making, to the best of my belief, a straight line across the marsh, as I had done hundreds of times before. But a mist is deceptive, and I could not have been walking more than a quarter of an hour when I felt the ground suddenly give way beneath me, and I found myself disappearing into one of the deep ditches that intersect the marsh between the broader dykes.

I knew that there was brackish water at the bottom of the ditch, and though I did not mind a ducking, I did not care for a ducking in dirty water, and so far from home. By clutching on to the docks and teazels on the bank, I managed to hold myself up and get my heels into the soil, and then with one spring I landed myself on the opposite bank. My petticoats would not escape Deborah's notice, but my feet were dry, and even my skirts would not attract immediate attention.

But how had I got to the ditch? and where was I now? Yes, I must have borne further to the left than I had intended; but it did not much signify—one way across the marsh was as good as another to me, and I had better keep to this side now, and go home under the lee of the hill. There would be the advantage that I might be able to find my little titlark gain. I whistled, for I could not see the dog, and presently my call was answered by a loud barking close in front of me, and, lifting up my face, I vaguely saw Taff chasing some larger object before him into the mist.

I knew at once that in coming to this side of the ditch I had landed myself among a herd of the cattle that had now taken up their summer quarters upon the marsh. I was not afraid of the cattle. I had seen them there ever since I had been a child, browsing in the warm weather: they were part of the land. But I wondered just where I had got to, and I stopped to think where the sea was, and where the dyke. Without these two landmarks I was somewhat bewildered. The cattle closed around me. They, too, seemed to be doubtful about something, but they kept their eyes on me. I wished Taff would not bark so.

I turned round, and once more began walking briskly in the direction which I thought was the right one. A great brown beast stood just in front of me. I had not noticed him before, but he had come up over a mound of the uneven marsh-land, and stood staring at me with head gently rocking. Up till now I had not had a moment's uneasiness, but I began to wonder whether the marsh cattle were always safe. I moved, and the bull moved too. Taff barked louder than ever, and the bull began to bellow softly. I was never so cross with the dog in my life, and I could not punish him, for I dared not take my eyes off the brown beast.

I moved forward till I had passed the place where the bull stood. But now it was worse than ever. The mist was so thick, and I had so entirely lost my way, that I dared not retreat backwards for fear of falling into an unseen dyke, and some of the dykes were deep at this time of the year. I began to run gently, but my heart failed me as I heard behind me the bull following, still bellowing softly. If I were only on the right road, there must be a gate soon, but I feared I was not on the right road. Taff kept running round in front of me, hindering my speed. I felt that the creature was gaining on me. I don't think I was ever so frightened before. I don't remember that my presence of mind ever so entirely failed me as it did on that day. But my legs seemed as though they were tied together. I stood still waiting, and then I think I must have fallen to the ground.

I knew that the bull must be close upon me, and it was no more than what I expected when I felt myself suddenly lifted up by the waist and flung to what seemed to me an immense distance through the air. For a moment I lay stunned. The bellowing of the bull, the barking of the dog, the murmur of the sea,—all mingled in my ears in one great booming sound. Then slowly I became conscious that there was a human presence beside me in the fog. I opened my eyes. I was lying close under a five-barred gate. The bull was on the other side of it; Taffy lay whining beside me; and over me stood a big, tall man, looking down at me quietly.

"Are you hurt, miss?" said he.

I struggled into a sitting posture, and pulled myself up on to my feet by the help of the gate.

"No, no, thank you," answered I. But my head was dizzy, and my arm ached dreadfully.

"I'm afraid I flung you over rather hard," said he. "But there wasn't time to do it nicely."

"You flung me over!" cried I, aghast.

"To be sure," answered he. "Did you think it was the bull?"

He gave a short laugh—scarcely a laugh, it was so very grim and quiet. But when he laughed, his smile was like a white flash—I remember noticing it. I gazed at him. Angry as I was—and I was absurdly, childishly angry—I could not help gazing at this man, who was able to take me up like a baby and fling me over a five-barred gate in a twinkling.

He was very broad and strong; his eyes were dark brown, his hair was black and curling, and so was his beard. He had neither a pleasant face nor a handsome face—until he smiled. I was not conscious at the time of any of these details; but there, in the fog, I thought he looked very imposing.

"I'm afraid, if it had been the bull, he would have flung you farther and hurt you more," said he. "You lay there very handy for him."

How I hated myself for having fallen to the ground!

"Come, Taff," said I, giving the dog a little kick, "get up."

The dog sprang to his feet with his tail between his legs. No wonder he was frightened and surprised. I had never done such a thing to him before. But I had a vague feeling that if he had not hindered me I should have got over the gate alone, and I was savage at the idea of having needed help from a man.

"Good evening to you," said I, curtly, nodding my head in the direction of the man, but without looking at him again.

"Good evening," answered he, raising his hat. "I hope you'll be none the worse for your fall."

I vouchsafed no answer to this speech, but strode on down the track as fast as my aching limbs and dizzy head would allow me to do. The sea murmured on the beach at my right. I could not see it for the fog, but I could hear it. After a while I think it must have lulled my anger to rest. The sea has always been a good friend to me, in its storms as in its calm. I like to see it rage as I dare not rage, and I like to see it calm as I cannot be calm. The restless sea has taught me as many things as the quiet marsh: they are both very wide. And that day I am sure it lulled my irritable temper.

Before long I began to think that I, to say the least of it, had treated my deliverer with scant courtesy. When I got to the farm that divides the marsh from the beach, I turned round to see if he were following. The fog was beginning to lift. The distant hills of the South Downs rose out of the sea of vapour, and were as towering mountains in the mystery, lying dim and yet blue against the struggling light of the sunset behind. The white headland that I had left, detached itself boldly against the sea-line—for the mist was only on the level land now, where it lay like a sheet a few feet above the marsh, so that the objects on the ground itself shone, illumined by the slanting rays of the sun, till each one had a value of its own in the scene. Through the golden spray of the sunlit vapour the red and the white cattle shone like jewels upon the brown land, where every little line of water was like a snake in the vivid light; and as I turned and looked towards the grey cliff, where I had climbed the bank after the bird's nest a few hours before, the long line of hill behind, dotted with fir-trees and church steeples and little homesteads, lay midway in the air through the silver veil.

I stood awhile looking back. I do not know that I was conscious of the wonder of the scene, but I remember it very vividly. At the time I think I was chiefly busy wishing the stranger to come up, that I might rectify my lack of courtesy. I saw him at last. He came in sight very slowly, and stood a long while leaning against the last gate lighting his pipe. I watched him several minutes, and he never once looked along the path to see if I was there. Why was I annoyed? I had dismissed him almost rudely. He did but do as he was bid. And yet I do believe I was annoyed: I do believe I was unreasonable to that point.

CHAPTER XIV.

When I came in to supper that evening, my friend of the fog was standing beside father on the parlour hearth-rug. Directly I saw him, I wondered how I could have been such a fool as not to have guessed at once that that was Mr Trayton Harrod. But it had never occurred to me for a moment; and when I recognised in the man to whom I had promised to be friendly, also the person who had presumed to take me by the waist and pitch me over a gate, all my bad temper of before swelled up within me worse than ever, and I felt as though it would be quite impossible for me even to be civil. And yet I had since promised somebody, even more definitely than I had promised Joyce, that I would do my best to make matters run smoothly.

For that very evening father had made

an appeal to my better feelings. It seems that while I had been out, Reuben Ruck and mother had had a real pitched battle. Mother had told him to do something in preparation for the arrival of the bailiff, which he had refused to do; and upon that mother had gone to father, and had said that it was absolutely necessary that Reuben should leave.

When I came home I had found father standing on the terrace in the sunset. It was a very unwise thing for him to do, for the air was chill. I wondered what had brought him out, and whether he could be looking for me. The little feeling of estrangement that had been between us since he had settled for the bailiff to come to the farm had given me a great deal of pain, and a lump rose in my throat as I saw him there watching me come up the hill. It was partly repentance for the feelings I had had towards him, partly hope that he was going to want me again as he used to do.

"Where have you been, lass?" said he, when I reached him. "You look sadly."

I laughed. The tears were near, but I laughed. My arm hurt me very much, and my head ached strangely; but I was so glad to hear him speak to me again like that.

"The mist has taken my hair out of curl," said I—"that's all. I have been down to the cliffs, to take old Warren some tea. Did you want me?"

"Yes," answered he. "I want to have a talk with you."

"Well, come indoors then," said I. "You know you oughtn't to be out so late."

We went into the study. Mother and Deb were getting supper ready in the front dwelling-room. There was no lamp lit; we sat down in the dusk.

"Your mother and Reuben have had a row, Meg," began father, with a kind of twinkle in his eye, although he spoke gravely.

"A row!" echoed I. "What about?"

"About Mr Trayton Harrod," answered father. "She wants me to send Reuben away."

"Send Reuben away!" cried I, aghast. "Why, it wouldn't be possible. There would be more harm done by the old folks going away than any good that would come of new folks coming, that I'll warrant."

"That's not the question," said father, tapping the table with his hand. "Mr Harrod has got to come, you know, and if the old folk don't like it, why, they'll have to go."

"There's one thing certain," added I,— "Reuben wouldn't go if he were sent away fifty times."

Father laughed — the first time I had heard him laugh for a fortnight.

"Well, he'll have to be pleasant if he does stay," said he.

"Oh, you none of you understand Reuben," said I. "He's not so stupid as you all think. He'll be pleasant if he thinks it's for our good that he should be pleasant. He wishes us well. But he'll want convincing first. And," I added, with a little laugh, "maybe I want convincing myself first."

And it was then that father appealed to my better feelings.

"Yes, Meg," said he, "I know that. I've seen that all along, and maybe it's natural. We none of us like strangers about. But I thought fit to have Mr Harrod come for the good of the farm, and now what we all have to do is to treat him civilly, and make the work easy for him." I was silent, but father went on. "And what I want you to do, Meg, is to help me make the work easy for him. It won't be easier to him than it is to us. If his father had not died beggared, I suppose he would have had his own by now. It is a hard thing for children when their parents beggar them." It being dark, I could not see his face, but I heard him sigh, and I saw him pass his hand over his brow. "Mother is right," he added. "We ought to make him feel it as little as we can; and as Joyce is away, you're the daughter of the house now, Meg. I want you to remember that. I want you to do the honours of the house as a daughter should. What a daughter is at home a wife will be when she is married."

"I shall never marry," said I, with a short laugh. "But I'll behave properly, father, never fear."

"That's right, my lass," said father, who seemed to take this speech as meaning something more conciliatory than it looks now as I set it down. "He is coming to-night to supper. Mother means to ask him to come every night to supper. She would have liked to give him house-room, but that don't seem to be possible. So we mean to make him welcome to our board."

"All right," said I. "I suppose mother knows best."

"Yes," echoed father; "mother always knows best. She's a wise woman—that's why every one loves her."

Again I promised to do what I could to resemble mother—to conciliate Reuben, and to make myself agreeable to our guest. And yet, alas! in spite of all that, I could not conquer my petty feelings of ill-temper when I came into the parlour and found that the man to whom I intended to be polite was the man who had offended me by being polite to me. What a foolish girl I was! As I look back upon it now, I am half inclined to smile. But I was only nineteen.

Mr Harrod had his back towards me when I came into the room. But I could not have failed to recognise the broad strong shoulders, and the very black curly hair. I must have been the more changed of the two, for

I had brushed and braided my locks, which curled all the merrier for the wetting, and I had put on another dress. Nevertheless his eyes had scarcely rested upon me before his mouth broke again into that smile that showed the strong white teeth.

" I hope you're none the worse, miss," said he. " I was afraid you had got a bad shaking."

Deborah, who was bringing in the supper, looked at me sharply. Mother had not yet come in, and father was in a brown study, but the remark had not escaped old Deb. She could not keep silence even before a stranger.

" I thought you looked as if you had been up to some mischief again," said she. " Your face is a nice sight."

I flushed angrily. I think it was enough to make any girl angry. It was bad enough to know that I was disfigured by a scratch on my cheek without having a stranger's attention attracted to it, and running a risk besides of a scolding from mother, who came in at the moment. Luckily she did not hear what Deborah had said. She was too much engaged in welcoming her guest, which she did with that gentle dignity that to some might have looked like a want of cordiality, but to me seems, as I look back upon it, to be just what a welcome should be—hospitable without being anxious. But when we were seated at the supper-table she noticed the mark on my face.

"It's only a fall that I got on the marsh," said I, in answer to her inquiry. "It isn't of the slightest consequence."

She said no more, neither did Mr Harrod. I must say I was grateful to him. He saw that I wished the matter to be forgotten, and he respected my desire, but I have often wondered since what construction he put upon my behaviour. If he thought about me at all, he must have considered me a somewhat extraordinary example of a young lady, but I do not suppose that he did consider me at all. Of course I was nothing but a figure to him: he had plenty to do feeling his level in the new life upon which he had just entered.

I am sure that Mr Harrod was a very shy and a very proud man. When mother said that she should expect him every evening to sup at the Grange, he refused her invitation with what I thought scant gratitude, although the words he used were civil enough; and when father spoke of his friendship with the Squire, he said that he was beholden to the Squire for his recommendation, but that he should never consider himself a friend of a man who was in a different station of life to himself.

I think in my heart I admired him for this sentiment, and father should also have approved of it; but, if I remember rightly, mother made some quiet rejoinder to the effect that it was not always the people who were on one's own level that were really one's best friends. I recollect that she, who was wont generally to sit and listen, worked hard that evening to keep up the conversation.

Dear mother! whom with the arrogance of youth I had never considered excellent excepting as a housewife or a sick-nurse. County news, the volunteer camp, the drainage of the marsh, the scarcity of well-water, the want of enterprise in the townspeople, the coming elections,—dear me, she had them all out; whereas father and I, who had undertaken, as it were, to put our best legs foremost, sat silent and glum. To do myself justice, I had a racking headache, and for once in my life I really felt ill, but I might have behaved better than I did.

Mr Harrod began to thaw slowly under the influence of mother's kindness. She had such a winning way with her when she chose, that everybody gave way before it; and I noticed that even from the very first, when he was certainly in a touchy frame of mind towards these, his first employers, Mr Harrod treated mother with just the same reverential consideration that every one always used towards her.

In spite of it all, that first evening was not a comfortable time. Father and Mr Harrod compared notes upon different breeds of cattle and upon different kinds of grains; but there was a restraint upon us all, and I think every one was glad when mother made the move from the table and father lit his pipe. I have no knowledge of how they got on afterwards over their tobacco: when I rose from the table the room swam around me, and if it had not been for

Deborah, who, entering on some errand at the moment, took me by the shoulders and pushed me out of the door in front of her, I am afraid I should have made a most unusual and undignified exhibition of myself in the Grange parlour. As it was, I had to submit to be tucked up in bed by the old woman, and only persuaded her with the greatest difficulty not to tell mother of my accident, some account of which, as was to be expected, she wrung from me in explanation of Mr Harrod's words in the parlour.

"I'd not have been beholden to him if I could have helped it," were the consoling words with which she left me; and as I lay there, aching and miserable, I became quite convinced that any comradeship between myself and my father's bailiff had become all the more impossible because of the occurrence of the afternoon.

END OF THE FIRST VOLUME.

PRINTED BY WILLIAM BLACKWOOD AND SONS.

www.ingramcontent.com/pod-product-compliance
Lightning Source LLC
Chambersburg PA
CBHW031939230426
43672CB00010B/1983